# MOVIE CLIPS
## FOR
## CREATIVE MENTAL HEALTH EDUCATION

by Fritz Engstrom, M.D.

# MOVIE CLIPS
## for Creative Mental Health Education

© 2004 by Wellness Reproductions & Publishing

International copyright protection is reserved under Universal Copyright Convention, and bilateral copyright relations of the U.S.A.

The original purchaser of this book is authorized to reproduce and use the individual items in this book for the generation of creative activity in a psychiatric / therapeutic / educational setting. However, this book may not be reprinted or resyndicated in whole or in part as a reproducible worksheet book or collection, or for any other purpose without the written permission of the publisher.

This publication is sold with the understanding that the publisher is not engaged in rendering psychological, medical or other professional services.

This publication is meant to be used by an ADULT facilitator only. The handouts/activities should be photocopied for distribution, or if this book contains a CD, they can also be printed.

Library of Congress Catalog Card Number: 2003116258
ISBN 10: 1-893277-24-0
ISBN 13: 978-1-893277-24-3

# Acknowledgements

I owe a tremendous debt of gratitude to so many people who have given generously to me for years. Patients, students, friends and colleagues encouraged and inspired me to use film clips to teach concepts of mental health. Over the course of 15 years, the Family Practice Residents at the University of Minnesota and my cohorts at Park Nicollet Clinic prodded me onward, and always suggested additional films to watch.

Several friends reviewed and edited portions of this book, including Catherine Brand, Stephanie Keep, Jane Schultz, Neil Ross and Lorin McLoughlin. Ann McCloskey and her daughter, Colleen (the comma queen) provided invaluable insights and ideas. My daughter, Anna, offered unsparing and brilliant editorial advice, as did my son, Carl and his wife, Kristin. They have improved the book significantly. I wish that my father, who was my first and most brutal editor, were alive to appreciate the manuscript.

Ellen patiently encouraged and prodded me for years, and her critiques made this book immeasurably better. She was a sure and perceptive sounding board. I dedicate this book to her.

My editors and publishers, Kathy Khalsa and Estelle Leutenberg, immediately understood the concept of the book, and crafted it into coherence.

With such assistance, you might imagine that the book is flawless. Alas, no amount of editorial assistance can transform me into a more insightful clinician, improve my prose or cause me to watch better movies. As a psychiatrist, I must blame my mother for my shortcomings. Just kidding – she is my biggest fan and I thank her for her love and support.

# Introduction

Who should read this book? Anyone who wants to know more about psychological distress and how to help or get help. The movie scenes, questions and discussion in this book help you understand the symptoms of mental problems, and how to think about them in the context of mental disorders. I will illustrate, using movie scenes, the process of making a diagnosis and naming common disorders so that we will have a common framework for discussion. The scenes also illustrate considerations for treatment: what to look for, when to beware, and how to evaluate progress.

Because movies are the closest that we have to a common culture, these scenes can be used by many groups. I have used them with the general public, psychiatric inpatients, mental health professionals, psychiatric residents, medical students, primary care physicians, seasoned psychiatrists, nurses, college students, psychology students, and professionals outside of medicine.

You can understand scenes from movies on several different levels; they are versatile. As a result, many professionals and nonprofessionals can appreciate and benefit from this book. Let's look at the scene from *The Hospital* as an example. Clinicians learning about diagnosis, especially clinicians in the fields of psychiatry and psychology, may focus on the symptoms of depression; social workers and others concerned with social dynamics may discuss the influence of family discord, mid-life crisis, social disintegration, and occupational difficulties on depression; chemical dependency counselors may highlight the interactions of alcohol, depression, and despair; patients, families and the general public may appreciate the experience of depression and how it influences several facets of life. Therapists of all types may debate which problem to address first: the alcohol, depression, rage, crumbling career, family tensions, or existential anguish. College psychology classes can use the book as a supplement to abnormal psychology classes, whereas high school health or psychology classes can use the book as a springboard to understand the interactions between individual, familial, occupational, and societal factors. An actor asked me to help her find a scene depicting panic attack so that she could prepare for an audition. Most scenes can be appreciated by several audiences; the questions are aimed primarily at patients or clients, the public, and friends and family members of those with mental disorders. The discussion sections are aimed toward every reader who wants to appreciate mental disorders and their treatment. The book is meant as a starting point, and not as a definitive tract on the issues that arise.

*Movie Clips for Creative Mental Health Education* is not comprehensive. I do not cover sexual disorders, childhood disorders, cultural diversity or several others. I focus on common disorders experienced by adults and it is intended to be a supplement to teaching rather than a definitive guide to diagnosis and treatment.

Too often, those who teach psychology and psychiatry rely solely on written or oral techniques. We use written and oral language to describe patients and to define treatment; the teaching may be dry and didactic. Contrast this to surgery, which is based on visual-motor descriptions and actions. Surgical texts are filled with pictures. Our mental health texts are rarely illustrated, except for some college texts of abnormal psychology.

# Introduction (continued)

Psychological terminology can be difficult, obscure and misleading. Pictures – movie scenes – can help us to clarify the confusing language of our fields. Movies are our common currency, our common language. Movies allow me to talk to people of diverse cultures. We have more of a common language through movies than we do through other venues such as politics, fiction or oral history.

In addition, we need to realize that *visual* images constitute our world of psychiatry and psychology. When I look at my patient in the lobby, watch her stand up, walk beside her to my office, and gaze on the tears running down her cheeks, I have learned more about her through my eyes than by listening to her description of the weather outside. As I listen to a man describe his wife's choking him, I hear the description of the horrible domestic scene but his smile betrays his relief that the marriage is finally over. This book is an attempt to balance the verbal with the visual aspects of the mental health fields. After viewing Cloris Leachman's depiction of Ruth Popper in *The Last Picture Show*, not only do you know the symptoms of Major Depression, but you can appreciate viscerally the experience of being depressed.

Psychologically, films offer a subtle advantage over other teaching tools. On the one hand, well-chosen scenes are gripping – more so than a dry lecture or even than a passage from a work of fiction. On the other hand, films offer enough distance so that individuals can discuss the problems that the people in the scene face without having to reveal their own struggles. Films respect psychological distance.

Filmmakers bring a fresh perspective. Within our mental health disciplines, we may see just what we are taught to see. One advantage of using films is that we see people and events through the eyes of someone who is not a mental health professional.

I believe that learning should be fun, and that we learn best if we are enjoying ourselves and are emotionally engaged. We need to enrich our teaching and enhance comprehension by using visual images. Sessions with patients are highly charged and engrossing — grim humor, voyeurism, unspeakable sadness, cruelty, and triumph exude from every session. Psychiatry is exciting, and that excitement may not be conveyed well by traditional oral and written material. Well-chosen movie scenes capture some of the excitement; they keep your interest and provoke spirited discussion.

I have chosen to use scenes rather than entire movies. From a practical point of view, I cannot show an entire movie during a 45-minute talk, nor can I expect patients or students to slog through several feature-length films. For the purposes of learning mental health topics, watching an entire movie has other drawbacks. People get caught up in the plot and may miss the teaching points. Many people react to a movie by saying that they liked it or did not like it, or they say that they liked the ending. Movies are complex, and it is hard to focus on a few key elements. Each of us remembers different aspects of the movie, so that a movie discussion can be frustrating. I find that brief scenes convey just the right amount of material. For example, the scene from *The Last Days of Disco* provokes discussion of Narcissistic Personality Disorder; we are not distracted by other themes in the film such as drug abuse, friendships, young adulthood or marginal employment. If we examine two to seven minute scenes we can engage in a valuable dialogue.

# Introduction (continued)

There are limitations to using films to understand psychiatry. Movies infrequently depict characters with clear-cut diagnoses. In that way, they are true to real life. Films depict characters with a variety of roles and characteristics. As a result, the scenes that I choose are the starting place for discussion, and are not meant to depict definitive diagnoses or disorders. Another limitation is that movies often show psychiatrists and other mental health professionals as evil, inept, comical, cruel or exploitive. Accordingly, the chapters on treatment are laced with scenes from movies that show what not to do, and how not to treat patients. These unflattering scenes often contain grains of truth; clinicians sometimes become overbearing, bored and self-centered.

I urge teachers and others who will use scenes from movies to build a collection of films on DVD or videocassette format. For years I rented films, and recently have begun purchasing them. You can purchase used videocassettes for a couple of dollars. I find that owning films is ultimately less expensive than renting them, and videocassettes can be cued up to the appropriate scenes so that they are ready for any teaching exercise. Owning 15 to 40 films will cost less than $150. I appreciate the convenience of using mail order rentals and the use of the local video store.

For each scene I give the timing — refer to How to Use This Book, page vii, "Find the Scene" section.

I love watching good movies, and I hope that this book conveys that love. When I lecture about psychiatry and use these scenes, audience members often choose to rent the entire movie. I am particularly fond of some of the forgotten or lesser-known films: *A Couch in New York, Brassed Off, Dressed to Kill, Lone Star, Manhattan Murder Mystery, Midnight Run* and *Truly Madly Deeply*. Singers try out their songs in front of live audiences before recording them, and writers often polish their material in essay or short-story format before writing a book. I lecture frequently, and have learned which movie scenes are illustrative and memorable.

# How to Use this Book

## THE FORMAT:

Explanation of the Chapter's Theme: The explanation page for each chapter orients readers to the themes developed in that chapter. As a result, the explanation page for section one in the first chapter includes the diagnostic criteria for depression, whereas the explanation page for chapter four gives an overview of the doctor-patient relationship, confidentiality, and boundaries.

## Each Movie Section Includes:

**1. Movie Information Page:** The first page of each film clip gives background about the film, actors and scene. The summary of the movie provides a context for the scene. The summary of the scene highlights some of the key teaching points in the scene. The facilitator or teacher may want to review this section to decide which scenes to use.

Find the Scene: Locate any scene on either a DVD or VHS formatted film. Each of the films can be rented; better yet, purchase used films from an on-line retailer or local video rental store for a few dollars. For each scene I give the timing - where to find the scene in relation to the title, as well as a comment about the start and end of the scene. As a result, the footage at the start of the cassette, which contains trailers and other advertisements, is not counted. Since I have not found any other book that uses movie scenes, I invented a system to tell readers how to find the scenes. Occasionally the DVD and videocassette timings do not coincide; I do not know why that occurs. I suspect that some films are edited between the time of the releases on videocassette and DVD. I hope that the descriptions of the scenes will allow the reader to find the scene without much difficulty. Please inform the publisher about errors so that I can correct future editions.

View the Scene: I recommend viewing the scene after reading the summary of the movie aloud. After viewing the scene, the group or class understands the issues; I am always impressed at the subtlety of the discussions that these provocative scenes elicit.

Note: I have included two scenes from three films (*Ordinary People, As Good As It Gets*, and *Broadcast News*). In the text, the first one is referred to as (1), and the second one as (2).

**2. Insight Page:** This page is intended to be used with clients or patients, to prompt them to think about themselves. Psychology students and others can answer these questions to probe their own psyches. Questions for students / staff prompt insight and understanding.

**3. Discussion Outline:**

Students / staff at all levels can appreciate nuances of diagnosis and treatment. Clinicians, faculty and teachers can use this section to lead discussions among students (or patients if appropriate).

## COPY THE PAGES:

The book's format allows you to photocopy the: (1) movie information, (2) insight questions and (3) discussion outline.

## ADDITIONAL READING:

I recommend that the reader refer to comprehensive texts for more extensive discussion of the issues. This book is not comprehensive, and other books will elucidate more completely issues of phenomenology, diagnosis, psychotherapy and medication.

# Table of Contents

**CHAPTER 1: Diagnosis Related**
  Section One: Depression . . . . . . . . . . . . . . . . . . . . . . . . . . . . . . . . . . . . . . . . . . . . .1
    *The Last Picture Show* . . . . . . MajorDepressive Disorder . . . . . . . . . . . . . . . . . . .3
    *Ulee's Gold* . . . . . . . . . . . . . Dysthymic Disorder . . . . . . . . . . . . . . . . . . . . . . .7
    *Brassed Off* . . . . . . . . . . . . . Adjustment Disorder with Depressed Mood . . . . . . . . . . .11
    *The Hospital* . . . . . . . . . . . Depression, Alcohol Abuse, Family Conflict, Life Circumstances . .15
  Section Two: Bipolar . . . . . . . . . . . . . . . . . . . . . . . . . . . . . . . . . . . . . . . . . . . . . . . .19
    *Lone Star* . . . . . . . . . . . . . Hypomanic Episode . . . . . . . . . . . . . . . . . . . . . . .21
    *Good Morning Vietnam* . . . . . Hypomania and Creativity . . . . . . . . . . . . . . . . . . . . .25
  Section Three: Schizophrenia . . . . . . . . . . . . . . . . . . . . . . . . . . . . . . . . . . . . . . . . . .29
    *A Beautiful Mind* . . . . . . . . Schizophrenia and Visual Hallucinations . . . . . . . . . . . . .35
    *Midnight Run* . . . . . . . . . . . Panic Attack . . . . . . . . . . . . . . . . . . . . . . . . . . . .39
    *Manhattan Murder Mystery* . . Panic Attack, Agoraphobia . . . . . . . . . . . . . . . . . . . .43
    *Broadcast News* (1) . . . . . . . . Performance Anxiety . . . . . . . . . . . . . . . . . . . . . . .47
    *Four Weddings and a Funeral* . Performance Anxiety, Stage Fright & Shyness . . . . . . . . . . .51
    *As Good As It Gets* (1) . . . . . Obsessive-Compulsive Disorder . . . . . . . . . . . . . . . . . .55
    *The Straight Story* . . . . . . . . Posttraumatic Stress Disorder and Substance Abuse . . . . . . . .59
  Section Five: Substance Abuse and Dependence . . . . . . . . . . . . . . . . . . . . . . . . . . . .63
    *28 Days* . . . . . . . . . . . . . . Alcohol and Drug Dependence, Enabling . . . . . . . . . . . . .65
    *Traffic* . . . . . . . . . . . . . . . Drug Dependence, Drugs and the Family . . . . . . . . . . . . .69
    *Clean and Sober* . . . . . . . . . A Sober Life . . . . . . . . . . . . . . . . . . . . . . . . . . . .73
    *Affliction* . . . . . . . . . . . . . Alcohol Dependence, Adult Child of Alcoholic . . . . . . . . . .77
  Section Six: Personality Disorders . . . . . . . . . . . . . . . . . . . . . . . . . . . . . . . . . . . . . .81
    *The Caine Mutiny* . . . . . . . . Paranoid Personality Disorder . . . . . . . . . . . . . . . . . .85
    *Cape Fear* . . . . . . . . . . . . . Antisocial Personality Disorder . . . . . . . . . . . . . . . . .89
    *Fatal Attraction* . . . . . . . . . Borderline Personality Disorder, Suicidal Behavior . . . . . . . .93
    *Play Misty For Me* . . . . . . . . Borderline Personality Disorder, Stalking . . . . . . . . . . . .97
    *Anywhere But Here* . . . . . . . Histrionic Personality Traits . . . . . . . . . . . . . . . . . . .101
    *The Last Days of Disco* . . . . . Narcissistic Personality Disorder . . . . . . . . . . . . . . . . .105
    *The Fisher King* . . . . . . . . . Avoidant Personality Disorder, Dependency, Depression . . . . . .109
    *Broadcast News* (2) . . . . . . . . Obsessive-Compulsive Personality Disorder . . . . . . . . . . . .113

**CHAPTER 2: Life Cycle Events**
  Section One: Bereavement and Pathological Grief . . . . . . . . . . . . . . . . . . . . . . . . . . .117
    *Saving Private Ryan* . . . . . . . Grief and Forgetting . . . . . . . . . . . . . . . . . . . . . . .119
    *Smoke* . . . . . . . . . . . . . . Pathological Grief, Visual Memories . . . . . . . . . . . . . . .123
    *Truly Madly Deeply* . . . . . . . Therapy for Pathological Grief . . . . . . . . . . . . . . . . . .127
  Section Two: Families and Life Crises . . . . . . . . . . . . . . . . . . . . . . . . . . . . . . . . . . . .131
    *Ordinary People* (1) . . . . . . . Family Conflict . . . . . . . . . . . . . . . . . . . . . . . . . .133
    *The Graduate* . . . . . . . . . . Coming of Age . . . . . . . . . . . . . . . . . . . . . . . . . .137
    *My Dinner With Andre* . . . . . Adult Developmental Issues, Intimacy, Fear of Death . . . . . . .141

**CHAPTER 3: Healing in Mental Health Settings** . . . . . . . . . . . . . . . . . . . . . . . . . . . . .145
    *Birdy* . . . . . . . . . . . . . . . Hospitalization . . . . . . . . . . . . . . . . . . . . . . . . .147
    *As Good As It Gets* (2) . . . . . The Right Medicine and a Good Doctor-Patient Relationship . . .151
    *E.T.* . . . . . . . . . . . . . . . Belief as a Therapeutic Tool . . . . . . . . . . . . . . . . . . .157

**CHAPTER 4: The Therapeutic Relationship** . . . . . . . . . . . . . . . . . . . . . . . . . . . . . . .161
    *Silence of the Lambs* . . . . . . Establishing the Doctor-Patient Relationship: Honesty . . . . . .163
    *Good Will Hunting* . . . . . . . Establishing the Doctor-Patient Relationship: Sincerity . . . . . .167
    *Ordinary People* (2) . . . . . . . Establishing the Doctor-Patient Relationship: Genuineness . . . .171
    *A Couch in New York* . . . . . . Warmth and Caring Can Overcome Poor Technique . . . . . . . .175
    *Dressed to Kill* . . . . . . . . . Boundaries, Psychiatrist Who Is Too Involved . . . . . . . . . .179
    *Frances* . . . . . . . . . . . . . . The Patient Who Is Famous, Self-Centered Doctor . . . . . . . .183
    *Grosse Point Blank* . . . . . . . Patient with Disturbing Background . . . . . . . . . . . . . . .187
    *Analyze This* . . . . . . . . . . . Psychiatrist Who Is Bored . . . . . . . . . . . . . . . . . . . .191

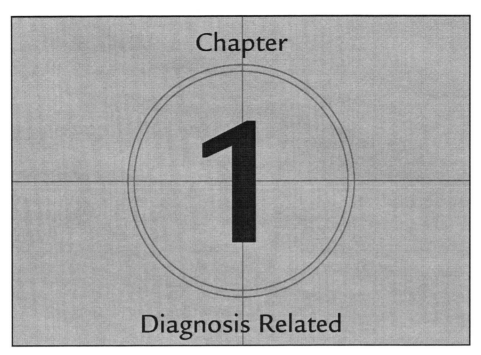

## Section One - Depression

*"When I say impotent, I mean I've lost even my desire to work. That's a helluva lot more primal passion than sex. I've lost my reason for being, my purpose. The only thing I ever truly loved."*

Dr. Herbert Bock
(George C. Scott) in *The Hospital*

**Movie Clips:**

| | |
|---|---|
| *The Last Picture Show* | Major Depressive Disorder |
| *Ulee's Gold* | Dysthymic Disorder |
| *Brassed Off* | Adjustment Disorder with Depressed Mood |
| *The Hospital* | Depression, Alcohol Abuse, Family Conflict, Life Circumstances |

# Definitions

## Chapter 1- Diagnosis Related - Section One

### Major Depressive Disorder

Five or more of the following symptoms have been present during the same 2-week period and represent a change from previous functioning. At least one of the first two symptoms is present.

    A. Depressed mood (it may be irritable mood in children or adolescents)
    B. Markedly diminished interest or pleasure in all or almost all activities (anhedonia)
    C. Significant increase or decrease in appetite, or significant weight loss (not due to dieting) or gain
    D. Insomnia or hypersomnia (excessive sleeping)
    E. Psychomotor agitation (antsiness / restlessness) or psychomotor retardation (slowing down / sitting like a lump)
    F. Fatigue or loss of energy
    G. Feelings of worthlessness or excessive or inappropriate guilt
    H. Diminished ability to think, concentrate, make decisions, or remember
    I. Recurrent thoughts of death, thoughts or plans for suicide, or suicide attempt

### Dysthymic Disorder

    A. Depressed mood for most of the day, more days than not, for at least two years.
    B. Presence, while depressed, of two or more of the following:
        1) Poor appetite or overeating
        2) Low energy or fatigue
        3) Insomnia or hypersomnia
        4) Low self-esteem
        5) Poor concentration or difficulty making decisions
        6) Feelings of hopelessness

# The Last Picture Show

**Date of Movie:** 1971

**Actors in this scene:** Timothy Bottoms as Sonny Crawford
Cloris Leachman as Ruth Popper

**Timing on DVD:**
| | | |
|---|---|---|
| 0:00:13 | Title |
| 0:23:20 | Start |
| 0:28:34 | End |

**Start of scene (VHS):** 0:22:12 after the title
Sonny drives a jalopy to Ruth's house.

**End of scene (VHS):** 0:27:07 after the title
Sonny leaves the kitchen; Ruth sits alone.

**Duration of scene:** 4:55

---

**Summary of Movie:**
*The Last Picture Show* is a bittersweet drama set in a small town in Texas in the 1950s. Sonny Crawford, an innocent teenage boy adrift in the shallowness and narrowness of adolescence, is exposed to an equally perplexing adult world of shifting mores and affections.

**Summary of Scene:**
Sonny is a high school student who has been asked by his gym teacher (the coach) to drive his wife to the doctor. Sonny drives her to the doctor, and he drives her home when the appointment ends. She asks him inside for a refreshment. Throughout the scene Ruth stares blankly ahead, hardly reacts to her surroundings, weeps unexpectedly, speaks with a hollow voice, and betrays no sense of joy. Sonny becomes increasingly uncomfortable in her presence, especially when she says that he has no idea why she is miserable.

## *The Last Picture Show*: Insight Questions

What symptoms of Major Depressive Disorder does Ruth Popper display? Which of these symptoms do you have? Have you ever known someone who had most or all of these symptoms?

In this scene, Sonny is very uncomfortable when Ruth cries. How do you feel when you are in the presence of a depressed person?

How do others treat you when you feel depressed?

Ruth Popper turned quite ugly at the end of the scene. How do angry, rageful or frustrating feelings contribute to your depression, or depression that you have witnessed in others?

Ruth feels misunderstood. What do you wish others would understand better about you, and what can you say or do to get them to understand you better?

# *The Last Picture Show*: Discussion Outline

What symptoms of Major Depressive Disorder (MDD) does Ruth Popper display?

- Depressed mood (crying)
- Feelings of worthlessness (she thinks that he does not want to spend time with her)
- Loss of energy (she seems weary)
- Psychomotor retardation (when the horn honks)
- Diminished ability to make decisions (whether to invite Sonny into the house)
- Hints of anhedonia (she seems joyless)
- Hints of poor appetite (she does not eat or drink)

How does Sonny Crawford feel when Ruth cries, and what does that tell
you about spending time with a depressed person?

Sonny stops drinking his Dr. Pepper, and he does not know if he should swallow or not. He seemingly does not want to do anything that will upset Ruth. He gets so uncomfortable that he wants to leave. He tries to make her feel better by offering an explanation for her behavior (that she misses her husband because of the basketball practice).

It is common to feel very uncomfortable with a depressed person. When you sit with someone who is profoundly depressed you may not know why he or she is so miserable; you may feel bewildered. As a result, you may feel awkward, and want to leave or to "make the person feel better." It is hard to sit and talk with someone who feels so awful.

One of the difficulties faced by a mental health professional is the requirement that one sit with depressed people for long periods of time without becoming depressed oneself.

How do you explain Ruth's behavior at the end of the scene, when she asks
Sonny to leave?

Sonny gave an incorrect explanation for her crying, and she snapped at him for being ignorant. Her remark captures the irritability that is part of depression, the anger that comes when someone does not understand the nature of the problem, and the despair that comes when others are not empathic with the pain.

Besides the acting, what contributes to the mood?

- The jalopy that Sonny drove
- The dusty and dried outdoors
- The lyrics and melody to the commercial and other tune on the radio that contrasted so sharply with the reality of their life
- The austere kitchen

What are some aspects of Cloris Leachman's acting that contributed to the power of the scene?

Her psychomotor retardation was extraordinary - when Sonny inadvertently beeped the horn, she did not even flinch. In addition, her weeping in the kitchen expressed such emptiness and pain that Sonny was dumbstruck. Her indecisiveness about asking him into the house had an extraordinary ring of truth. Finally, her self-loathing and sense of worthlessness became evident when she said that he probably did not want to spend any time with her. Cloris Leachman captured these nuances seemingly effortlessly; she was believable.

# Ulee's Gold

| | |
|---|---|
| **Date of Movie:** | 1997 |
| **Actors in this scene:** | Peter Fonda as Ulee Jackson |
| | Patricia Richardson as Connie Hope |

**Timing on DVD:**

| | |
|---|---|
| 0:00:40 | Title |
| 0:54:30 | Start |
| 0:60:09 | End |

**Start of scene (VHS):**  0:53:52 after the title
"What's the word for beekeeper?" A scene in the kitchen.

**End of scene (VHS):**  0:59:31 after the title
"Keep me posted." Connie leaves.

**Duration of scene:**  5:39

---

**Summary of Movie:**
Ulee Jackson is a close-lipped beekeeper who raises his son's children. His orderly life is disrupted when he gets word from his imprisoned son that the son's wife is in trouble. Ulee has to find emotional and physical resources that he has never used.

**Summary of Scene:**
Ulee speaks with his neighbor about his struggles. He fought in the Vietnam War, his wife died, and he raises his grandchildren alone. He moves slowly, he stares, he is nearly expressionless when he is not tearful, he speaks in a soft voice with little animation, and his words and kitchen both bespeak low self-esteem. He talks about bees more easily than he speaks about his feeling of hopelessness and defeat.

# *Ulee's Gold*: Insight Questions

Ulee seems quite unhappy. When you are blue or depressed, what do others notice? What symptoms do you reveal?

Ulee mentions fighting in Vietnam, his wife's death, and raising grandchildren. What do you believe causes depression: difficult life events (stressors) or the way that people cope with life events?

Ulee raises his grandchildren. What are some of the challenges of being a single parent?

If you feel depressed, how does your depression impact on children that you raise or with whom you come in contact?

Ulee is a successful beekeeper. In what way does work allow you to develop and enhance personal relationships, and in what way is work an escape from people?

# *Ulee's Gold*: Discussion Outline

**What symptoms of Dysthymic Disorder (Dysthymia) does Ulee show?**

It is hard to be certain based on this scene, but my guess, based on Ulee's language, tone of voice, and body language, is that he has:

- Depressed mood
- Fatigue
- Low esteem
- Feelings of hopelessness

**What aspects to his tone of voice and body language suggest that he is depressed?**

The DSM IV, which describes symptoms, does not describe the subtler aspects of depression. Ulee has a soft, almost flat tone of voice. He walks slowly. He does not seem very animated. He seems fatigued. His shoulders are hunched over. His voice inflection drops when he talks. He never gets excited or animated.

**How do you feel when you are in the presence of Ulee?**

I feel depressed. I feel weary. I want to avoid him, since he brings a pessimistic attitude with him.

**What does that say about the social life of those who are depressed?**

- Depressed people often avoid other people – out of weariness, disinterest, low esteem or anger.
- Other people often desire to avoid depressed people, because of the contagious effect of depressed feelings.
- As a result, the social relationships that are necessary to help people get out of depression are often thwarted by the very nature of depression and its effect on others.

**One aspect of Dysthymia is that it lasts at least two years. Do you think that Ulee has been depressed for two years?**

Peter Fonda infuses Ulee with a shroud of hopelessness that feels pervasive. I do not know how Mr. Fonda does it, but I feel in my bones that Ulee could have been depressed for years and years. He does not show any sense of humor or even irony. When I see anger or sarcasm in a patient, I have the sense that the person may have enough spark to grapple with the depression. Ulee does not show that energy, and therefore I find it entirely plausible that he may have suffered from this depression for a long time. I would definitely consider prescribing an antidepressant, in addition to psychotherapy.

*(continued on page 10)*

## What causes Ulee's depression?

We do not have information about Ulee's genetics or about his early life experiences. However, this scene suggests that several stressors affect Ulee. These include:

- His wife's death
- His experiences in Vietnam
- Concern, hurt and anger about his son's imprisonment
- Isolation from adults
- A solitary occupation
- The burden of raising difficult grandchildren alone (acting as a single parent)
- Concern about his drug-addicted daughter-in-law

# Brassed Off

**Date of Movie:** 1996

**Actors in this scene:**
Stephen Tompkinson as Phil
Melanie Hill as Sandra
Ewan McGregor as Andy
Pete Postlewaite as Danny

**Timing on DVD:**
0:01:38     Title
1:17:55     Start
1:23:50     End

**Start of scene (VHS):**
1:28:58 after the title
Andy walks into the hospital and says, "All right Phil."

**End of scene (VHS):**
1:34:53 after the title
"Course he is, he's my dad."

**Duration of scene:** 5:55

**Summary of Movie:**
This politically charged film depicts the consequences of the British government's decision to close several coal mines. Many of the mines had their own brass bands, and the existence of these bands is also threatened. The struggle to keep the mine open parallels the struggles to keep the band playing and to keep the dignity, pride and spirit of the miners and their families intact.

**Summary of Scene:**
The mine is about to close, and Phil spent his last 50 pounds on a new trombone, despite his wife's firm instructions to the contrary. His furniture is repossessed, his father (who is also the bandleader) is stricken ill, he is humiliated and assaulted, and his wife and children abandon him. Prior to seeing his father he makes an inappropriate joke about his navel. He visits his father in the hospital but cannot bring himself to tell his father that he plans to quit the band. He cannot look his father in the eye. He returns to his empty apartment. He performs one of his odd jobs, which is to be a clown for children's parties. While performing for the children he launches into a vulgar political tirade, blasphemes his religion, and expresses despair and self-hatred. He states that he has lost the will to win, the will to fight, the will to live, and the will to breathe. He believes he has lost everything. He attempts suicide by hanging himself in a grotesque scene that mirrors his self-image.

# *Brassed Off*: Insight Questions

Phil acted inappropriately at a birthday party for children and shortly thereafter attempted suicide. What clues do people give that they are contemplating or planning suicide?

Phil expressed rage toward the English government. In your life, in what way is rage or intense anger related to depressed or suicidal feelings?

Phil believes that he has disappointed his ill father. Describe one episode in which you let down or disappointed a parent; how did you feel about yourself?

Phil's suicide attempt may have been related to feeling hopeless. How do you define hopeless?

Phil hung himself but did not die; similarly, many people attempt suicide but only a fraction of them die. List reasons why someone would attempt suicide but not want to die.

# *Brassed Off*: Discussion Outline

**What stressors does Phil struggle with in his life that might drive him to despair?**

Not all of these stressors are evident from the clip, but they include:
- He is losing his job, with the closing of the coal mine
- His father is dying
- Financially, he is not able to provide for himself and his family
- His wife left him
- The brass band will likely have to disband
- He is losing his apartment

**Are losses a common theme for those who experience depression?**

Yes, losses are commonly associated with depression. The losses noted above are tangible; intangible losses also contribute to depression:
- Loss of self-esteem
- Loss of role as provider
- Loss of role as head of the household
- Loss of a way of life
- Loss of identity as an excellent trombone player
- Loss of the fun and camaraderie as part of a band
- Loss of stature in the community

**Can you see anger or rage as part of his mood, in addition to the depression?**

This scene compares to the scene from *The Hospital*, page 15. Both Phil and Dr. Bock experience rage, and the targets of their rage are difficult to pin down. Phil makes inappropriate, sarcastic comments about the English government during a clown show for children.

*(continued on page 14)*

13

**How did he act just prior to his suicide attempt? Is there a connection between very odd behavior and suicide?**

His action at the birthday party was weird. His clown outfit and make-up added to the surrealistic atmosphere. Also, his friend was unable to console him, and he did not tell his father the truth about the band. His wife left him. He was socially isolated and expressed his anger in a way that he alienated more people.

The dialogue at the end of the scene sums it up:

**Nurse:** Is this man bothering you?

**Phil:** 'Course he is. He's me dad.

Highly suicidal people may act quite oddly once they have decided to take action. They may ignore the usual societal niceties, since they plan to depart that society soon. On the other hand, some people act happy and pleasant once they decide to commit suicide. The outward happiness may convince others not to watch them too carefully, may express the relief that comes from the decision to die, and may be part of an effort to repair broken relationships at the end of life.

# The Hospital

**Date of Movie:** 1971

**Actors in this scene:** George C. Scott as Dr. Herbert Bock
Diana Rigg as Barbara Drummond

**Timing on DVD:**
| | |
|---|---|
| 0:02:45 | Title |
| 0:47:40 | Start |
| 0:53:59 | End |

**Start of scene (VHS):** 0:44:55 after the title
Seated in a dark office, Dr. Bock tells Barbara, "You're wasting your time. I've been impotent for years."

**End of scene (VHS):** 0:51:14 after title
Dr. Bock says, "Close the door and turn out the lights on your way out."

**Duration of scene:** 6:19

---

**Summary of Movie:**
George C. Scott portrays an aging, brilliant, despairing doctor who tries to keep his urban hospital afloat in the midst of chaos. He confronts healthcare workers on strike, incompetent staff, and unexpected patient deaths.

**Summary of Scene:**
Barbara Drummond arrives at Dr. Bock's office late at night. He launches into a profound and protracted monologue exposing his physical and spiritual impotence, his drinking, his tortured family relationships, and his professional failures.

## *The Hospital*: Insight Questions

Does alcohol make you feel better or worse? How does the amount of alcohol relate to how it makes you feel? Does it ever cause you to feel depressed?

Dr. Bock conducted important medical research, yet now dismisses it or does not value it. Why might you or a depressed person not care about past achievements?

Dr. Bock mentions his sexual impotence. How does depression affect sexual functioning, and how do antidepressants affect sexual functioning?

Dr. Bock had an ugly falling out with his son. Have you ever felt alienated from a close family member? What factors contributed to the alienation?

Dr. Bock is furious both at himself and at the world that he inhabits. In what ways do you have a similar tendency to feel anger both inward (at yourself) and outward (toward others)?

© 2004 Wellness Reproductions & Publishing 1.800.669.9208

# *The Hospital*: Discussion Outline

What is the relationship between depression and alcohol? [See A through D below]

A. Are people who are dependent on alcohol (alcoholics) more likely than the average person to develop depression?

Alcoholics are more likely than other people to develop depression. That is not to say that alcoholism causes depression. Alcoholism <u>may</u> cause depression, presumably by dulling the brain, but that is only one possibility. Unknown genetic and / or biochemical factors may make people liable to develop both conditions, for example, by predisposing someone to feel awful, which in turn leads some people to drink to ease the emotional pain. Another possibility is that family upbringing "teaches" people to deal with life's troubles by drinking or by giving up.

B. Are depressed people more likely than other people to develop alcoholism?

Yes, depressed people develop alcoholism more often than others. Alcoholism may be one way to deal with depression. Or, the factors in the above paragraph (genetics, family environment) may be important. We do not know why, but depression and alcoholism travel together in many people.

C. Does untreated depression make it harder for an alcoholic to remain sober?

Yes. Recovering alcoholics (i.e., those alcoholics who are sober and committed to sobriety) who stop their antidepressants (and whose antidepressants successfully treated their depression), have a high rate of return of depression as well as a return to drinking.

D. Does drinking alcohol reduce the effectiveness of antidepressants?

Yes. It has been well documented that alcohol reduces the effectiveness of antidepressants. The degree of the effect is controversial. One study indicates that even moderate social use of alcohol reduces the effectiveness of antidepressants, whereas many psychiatrists feel that moderate use of alcohol (defined by some as up to three drinks per week, and others as one drink per day) does not interfere with the antidepressant action. All agree that alcohol abuse or dependence makes it nearly impossible for antidepressants to work.

Some doctors recommend no alcohol until the antidepressant works, and then moderate use after that. However, if someone is alcoholic, s/he should not attempt even moderate drinking.

*(continued on page 18)*

## What about Dr. Herbert Bock? What other factors seem to be involved with his depression?

- His relationship to his son.
- His relationship to his mother.
- His frustration at the direction his career has taken.
- Perhaps his intellectual decline.
- His sexual impotence.
- His isolation from others; his arrogance makes it hard to have intimacy or warm relationships with others.
- His despair at the current state of his hospital and community.

## Do these factors cause his depression, or does his depression make it harder to face these difficulties?

No one knows the answer to that question, and it is important to recognize the difficulty answering it. Sometimes when depression clears up, the factors that seem to be causes of depression no longer feel overwhelming, and can be handled readily. Sometimes just the opposite is true - no matter what antidepressant is given, until the difficulties are faced and dealt with, the depression and despair will remain.

## Is rage or anger a common emotion in those with depression?

One symptom of both Major Depressive Disorder and of Dysthymic Disorder is depressed mood, which is often summarized as "sad, blue or down in the dumps." However, it is often not appreciated that irritability or anger are other ways that people experience a depressed mood. Teenagers, children and men seem especially prone to irritability or anger as part of their depression.

## What do you make of George C. Scott's portrayal of Dr. Herbert Bock?

As a psychiatrist, and as a moviegoer, I find his performance compelling. This monologue captures the interweaving of rage and despair I often see in embittered and depressed doctors and other professionals. He convincingly moves from inner contempt (impotence, crumbling family) to rage at the outside world. At the same time that he anguishes over his bleak world, he grasps for self-esteem by remembering his previous academic success. I sense that he tries to cope with his despair by holding onto his memories, by throwing himself into his work, and by being a decent role model to the medical staff. I also appreciate that his powerful stature intimidates and distances those people in his life – his colleagues and family – whom he needs most. His behavior is self-defeating, which is typical of many who experience depression.

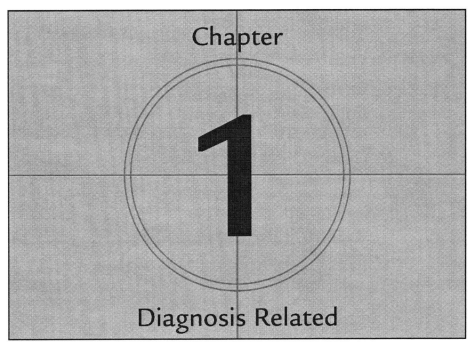

## Section Two - Bipolar Disorder

*"With me it was always 'high strung . . . or jumpy."*

Bunny
(Frances McDormand) in *Lone Star*

---

**Movie Clips:**

*Lone Star* . . . . . . . . . . . . . . . . Hypomanic Episode
*Good Morning Vietnam* . . . . . . . Hypomania and Creativity

# Definitions

## Chapter 1- Diagnosis Related - Section Two

### What is Bipolar Disorder?

It is the name of a disorder that consists of high periods (which are called Manic or Hypomanic episodes), low periods (episodes of Major Depression), and normal periods, in any order. Bipolar Disorder is also called Manic Depressive Illness. Refer to Chapter 1, Section One for the criteria for Major Depressive Episode.

### Manic Episode

A. A distinct period of abnormally and persistently elevated, expansive, or irritable mood lasting at least **one week**.

B. During the period of mood disturbance, three or more of the following symptoms to a significant degree:
   1) Inflated self-esteem or grandiosity
   2) Decreased need for sleep
   3) More talkative than usual or pressure to keep talking
   4) Flight of ideas or subjective experience that thoughts are racing
   5) Distractibility
   6) Increase in goal-directed activity or agitation [hyperactive]
   7) Excessive involvement in pleasurable activities that have a high potential for painful consequences: spending, sex, investments

### Hypomanic Episode

A. Same as A and B above, except for duration of only **four days**.

B. The episode is not severe enough to cause marked impairment or to necessitate hospitalization, and there are no psychotic features.

# Lone Star

| | |
|---|---|
| **Date of Movie:** | 1996 |
| **Actors in this scene:** | Chris Cooper as Sam<br>Frances McDormand as Bunny |
| **Timing on DVD:** | 0:03:15 Title<br>1:45:29 Start<br>1:50:04 End |
| **Start of scene (VHS):** | 1:42:15 after the title<br>A football game is on the television, and the announcer talks about the Texas Aggies. |
| **End of scene (VHS):** | 1:46:50 after the title<br>"Thanks, I like it when you say that, Sam." |
| **Duration of scene:** | 4:35 |

**Summary of Movie:**
The sheriff in this small Texas border town investigates the murder of a brutal former sheriff. The complex social and family history unfolds.

**Summary of Scene:**
Sam visits his ex-wife, Bunny, because he wants to review some old documents that shed light on his parents' past, and indirectly on an old murder. Bunny hopes that his visit signals his renewed interest in her and hopes that he has come back for her. Her apartment is adorned with football memorabilia, she talks incessantly about the local football teams despite Sam's evident lack of interest in football, she talks mostly about herself and her own interests, and she does not answer questions directly. Her emotions shift rapidly from elation to pathetic sadness; she is hyperactive, she makes an inappropriate remark about stool samples, and she alludes to taking medicine and being disciplined for setting fires.

## *Lone Star*: Insight Questions

Have you ever been around someone like Bunny, who spoke too much and too fast, and who did not make sense all the time? What did it feel like?

To be psychotic means to be out of touch with reality. Have you ever talked to a person exhibiting psychosis? If so, were you successful in convincing that person to embrace reality and to give up psychotic beliefs?

Sam seemed to walk on eggshells – he did not want to upset her. He gently asked whether she is still taking her medicine. How do you approach someone who is very high strung and easily angered?

Bunny is preoccupied with the college football team. What is the difference between being a good fan, and being excessively preoccupied (or even psychotic) about a football team? Is there a clear way to know the difference, or is it a judgment call?

Do you think Bunny needs medicine, and why?

# *Lone Star*: Discussion Outline

## Does Bunny experience symptoms of mania or hypomania?

- She is more **talkative** than usual.
- She seems to have a **pressure** to keep talking.
- One subject reminds her of another, and she thus has loosely connected thoughts in what is labeled **flight of ideas**. One idea seems to fly toward another partly related idea. She will go from one partially complete thought or idea to another.
- She relates to football stars, thus suggesting **grandiosity**. Her unusual décor and dress also suggest grandiosity, or at least flamboyance and tastelessness.
- She seems easily **distracted**, and does not answer Sam's queries.
- Her flitting about the room suggests **psychomotor agitation**.
- We strongly suspect that the symptoms have caused marked impairment in functioning, since her father has had to set limits on her, even though she is an adult; and she has set fires.

## Does Bunny experience psychosis?

Someone who is psychotic is out of touch with reality. When Bipolar Disorder is severe, patients become psychotic.

Bunny gives at least three hints that she may be psychotic. First, she is excessively concerned with football, even when her visitor shows no interest in the subject. Second, she mentions that recruiters test stool samples from football players, which seems bizarre and inappropriate. Third, she is preoccupied with the idea that athletes lift 350-pound weights, and gets upset that she may not be able to handle a weight on top of her.

Her mention of the fight at the football stadium could also suggest a psychotic process, since she was out of control. Saying that she wanted to sit in the cheap seats with real football fans also has the hint of psychotic thinking.

## What do you make of Bunny's sadness?

People in the throes of mania or hypomania are not always euphoric. As the diagnostic criteria suggest, patients may also be irritable. In addition, they may experience highly variable or even volatile mood changes. Sadness, euphoria, anger and rage may be interspersed with one another. If the sadness is pronounced, then Bunny may be described as having a mixed episode of Bipolar Disorder.

Her sadness has a particular quality. I find it hard to empathize with her sadness, since it seems unrelated to a seriously sad event. Instead, the sadness seems superficial, which is common for those with Bipolar Disorder. Contrast the empathic feeling that you have (or do not have) with Bunny with your feelings for Dr. Bock (*The Hospital*, page 15) or Phil (*Brassed Off*, page 11).

*(continued on page 24)*

## Do you think that Frances McDormand's character, Bunny, is realistic?

I believe that Ms. McDormand's portrayal of a manic or hypomanic woman is extraordinary. I have worked with patients who act and talk like her. In fact, it is the most convincing portrait of Bipolar Disorder that I have seen in the movies.

My difficulties with patients like Bunny are similar to those experienced by Sam. It is hard to get a word in edgewise. I find myself talking about topics that come out of the blue. I am laughing and smiling for no particularly good reason. I have a hard time staying focused on the subject at hand. And I am often the victim of shifting moods, including wrath. I have to be firm if I want to be understood, and hypomanic people do not take subtle hints.

# Good Morning Vietnam

**Date of Movie:** 1987

**Actors in this scene:**
Robin Williams as Adrian Cronauer
Forest Whitaker as Edward Garlick
Bruno Kirby as Lt. Steven Hauk

**Timing on DVD:**
| | |
|---|---|
| 0:00:34 | Title |
| 0:11:47 | Start |
| 0:18:47 | End |

**Start of scene (VHS):** 0:11:15 after the title
Green light turns off, red light turns on. Adrian says, "Good Morning Vietnam."

**End of scene (VHS):** 0:18:18
Adrian turns the show over to ". . . Dan Levitan."

**Duration of scene:** 7:03

---

**Summary of Movie:**
Adrian Cronauer is an army disc jockey in Vietnam in 1965 whose uproarious and irreverent monologues shake up the army brass and amuse the troops. His conflicts with the army and sympathies for the downtrodden are fairly predictable, but the monologues carry the film.

**Summary of Scene:**
On his first morning on the job, Adrian Cronauer hits high gear as disc jockey. He plays banned music by Martha and the Vandellas, makes sly sexual and racial references, satirizes the conflict (a jack-knifed water buffalo is tying up traffic on the Ho Chi Minh trail), undertakes a phony interview with a hard-of-hearing artilleryman, and portrays an effeminate fashion consultant who believes that the army should design fatigues that clash with their surroundings.

# *Good Morning Vietnam*: Insight Questions

Adrian Cronauer speaks very fast. How can you tell if someone is just funny and quick-witted versus mentally ill and talking abnormally fast?

Do you believe that people with psychiatric disorders are more creative and funny than people who do not have disorders? Why or why not?

One aspect of Adrian's humor is his ability to relate two seemingly unrelated events; he imagines a traffic jam (due to a water buffalo) on the Ho Chi Minh Trail, and he has an imaginary discussion with an effeminate fashion consultant about army clothing. Do you use humor to deal with terrible situations? If so, in what way?

Adrian's monologue amuses the soldiers but enrages his superiors. Do you feel that your supervisor, boss or leader stifles you and prevents you from being creative? How do you deal with that?

Adrian made jokes about the war, and his superior objected. When has your sense of humor been destructive, and when does it backfire?

# *Good Morning Vietnam*: Discussion Outline

### Does Adrian Cronauer have flight of ideas?

This scene portrays **flight of ideas** better than any that I have seen in films. It also shows how the **pursuit of a highly pleasurable activity** – in this case, doing a humorous riff on the radio – can be taken to a self-destructive extent. Clearly, his job is in jeopardy, and he may be court-martialled. Often, people with Bipolar Disorder are a lot of fun, but their humor wears thin because they do not know when to stop. It has been said that you can always tell who is manic in the psychiatric hospital - it is the person whom everyone loves the first day and hates thereafter.

### Are creative people often mentally ill?

Manic patients can be highly creative and funny. One study[1] found that many poets and other artists frequently suffer from Bipolar Disorder. I am unaware of a more recent study evaluating stand-up comics, but I would not doubt that several of them have Bipolar Disorder.

### Do you think that Adrian Cronauer has Bipolar Disorder?

Despite the above comments, I doubt that Adrian Cronauer would be diagnosed as having Bipolar Disorder in real life. He is able to turn his humor and flight of ideas on-and-off whenever he wants to do so. He is not constantly chattering when he is in other situations. In true mania and hypomania, the abnormal behavior persists in many settings. He does not display the symptoms of mania for a sustained period of time. Nonetheless, a careful interview could clarify additional symptoms, and would clarify whether he has experienced previous episodes of depression and / or mania. If he had never experienced an episode of major depression, then I would not diagnose him with Bipolar Disorder. He could also be evaluated for Attention-Deficit / Hyperactivity Disorder.

---

[1]Goodwin, Frederick and Jamison, Kay: "Manic-Depressive Illness, Creativity and Leadership," pp. 332-367, in Manic-Depressive Illness, New York, Oxford University Press, 1990

28

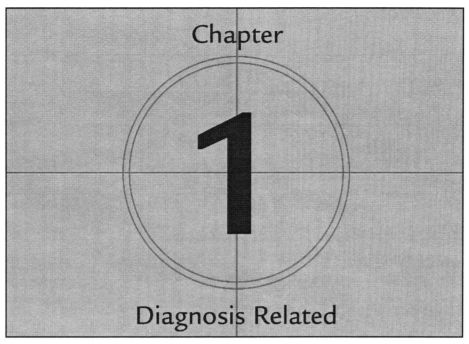

# Section Three - Schizophrenia

*"Is that what you are, soldier, some useless ghoul? The local madman?"*

Parcher
(Ed Harris) in *A Beautiful Mind*

| **Movie Clips:** |
|---|
| *A Beautiful Mind* . . . . . . . . . . . Schizophrenia |

# Definitions

## Chapter 1- Diagnosis Related - Section Three

### Schizophrenia

A. Two or more of the following symptoms:
1) Delusions (false, fixed beliefs)
2) Hallucinations (abnormal perceptions, especially auditory ones)
3) Disorganized speech
4) Grossly disturbed or catatonic behavior
5) Negative symptoms including flat affect (blank emotions), lack of motivation, or poverty (lack of) of speech

B. Dysfunction in the social and occupational sphere, continuous duration for at least six months, lack of significant depressive or manic symptoms, and not caused by substance abuse.

# A Beautiful Mind

**Date of Movie:**      2001

**Actors in this scene:**      Russell Crowe as John Nash
Ed Harris as Parcher
Josh Lucas as Martin Hansen

**Timing on DVD:**
| | |
|---|---|
| 0:05:20 | Title |
| 1:49:17 | Start |
| 1:50:28 | End |

**Start of scene (VHS):**      1:47:58 after the title
Two men leave an office, and one says, "This guy tries to wander into the library.."

**End of scene (VHS):**      1:49:09
Parcher says, "Ladies and gentlemen, the great John Nash."

**Duration of scene:**      1:11

---

**Summary of Movie:**
This film chronicles the life of John Nash, a Nobel-prize-winning mathematician from Princeton who develops Schizophrenia. The film depicts his visual hallucinations and delusions brilliantly, as well as the devastating impact of the illness on Nash's social and family life. His struggles with the treatments of the day – medicine and insulin shock therapy – are quite realistic.

**Summary of Scene:**
John Nash has just returned to Princeton on a part-time basis and has had an unfortunate incident in the library. His colleague notices that he is in a frenzy in the courtyard, as he charges around in agitation, and speaks to an imaginary person (Parcher, who is dressed in dark clothes, is a hallucination). The hallucination taunts Nash, telling him that he was once a great soldier, but is now reduced to a "useless ghoul . . . in a cell . . . old worthless, discarded . . . the world will burn to ashes . . . " John Nash argues with this menacing hallucination, and he protests that he is not a soldier, that there is no mission, and that Parcher is not real. The bystanders are bewildered and frightened, while his friend Martin tries to comfort him. John Nash walks away stiffly, alone, bewildered, and terrified.

# A Beautiful Mind: Insight Questions

What is the definition of a hallucination, and how real is Parcher to Nash? How easy is it to convince Nash that Parcher is not real?

How connected is Nash to the people around him? What is the effect of John Nash's hallucinations on those around him?

Nash smokes a cigarette. Is it usual for people with Schizophrenia to smoke cigarettes?

The content of the hallucinations involves being a soldier with an important mission. Why would someone be paranoid about being a soldier on a mission?

At the end of the scene Martin comforts John, and says something about being sorry about what just happened (perhaps alluding to an incident in the library). Does stress affect those with Schizophrenia?

32

© 2004 Wellness Reproductions & Publishing 1.800.669.9208

# *A Beautiful Mind*: Discussion Outline

## Do you think that Nash has Schizophrenia?

I believe that this is an excellent depiction of Schizophrenia. The presence of Parcher suggests auditory (Parcher talks) and visual (Parcher is visible to Nash) hallucinations. Talking about missions suggests delusions.  His speech is hard to understand when he is in a frenzy. His agitation indicates grossly disturbed behavior. His emotions seem flattened.

The distinction between Bipolar Disorder and Schizophrenia is controversial. The chief distinguishing characteristic between the two is the presence of depressed and manic moods in Bipolar Disorder, and the swing between these two states. In contrast, the essence of Schizophrenia is delusions and hallucination.  In this movie, it seems clear to me that the delusions and hallucinations account for most of the distress, and the mood problems are secondary to those psychotic symptoms. In conclusion, I believe that John Nash has Schizophrenia.

## What do you make of Parcher, the visual and auditory hallucination that menaces Nash?

This movie did an extraordinary job depicting hallucinations and delusions. In other scenes we see a sweet little girl, who is another of his hallucinations.

Many people have a hard time grasping the nature of hallucinations and delusions, and this film may educate them. One can see that Parcher (hallucination) does not readily go away, and that Nash cannot make him leave. He is very real to Nash. Similarly, delusions are false, fixed beliefs, and they do not vanish when someone wishes them to leave.

Parcher is accusatory, belittling, taunting, and menacing. Psychiatrists are less concerned with the nature of hallucinations than they once were, although Nash would be labeled as having the paranoid type of Schizophrenia, since the hallucinations are persecutory and grandiose. I say grandiose, since the theme is grand - being a soldier on a mission.

As in this film, delusions and hallucinations can cause people to act dangerously; people have been known to commit murder, suicide, and many other violent acts when responding to hallucinations.

## How does Nash relate to the people around him?

The people in the courtyard, and even his friend Martin, seem shut out. Nash is in a world of his own, and others are bystanders. He is not connected. He relates more intensely to his hallucination than to the real people in his life. He does not sob, warm up, or connect to those around him.

*(continued on page 34)*

This social isolation and disconnection from others is a prominent characteristic of those with Schizophrenia. In fact it is a feature that distinguishes Schizophrenia from Bipolar Disorder. Prior to 1980, most patients in the United States who developed psychotic symptoms were labeled as having Schizophrenia. When lithium was introduced in 1969, it became very important to distinguish Schizophrenia from Bipolar Disorder, since lithium could help those with Bipolar Disorder but not those with Schizophrenia. One of my mentors in medical school participated in the early studies of lithium, and he noticed a very interesting phenomenon. Patients with Bipolar Disorder were very engaged with people and often greeted the doctor at the door, whereas those with Schizophrenia sat alone and rarely made social contact with the doctor or with others. To this day, that distinction is valid and useful.

Subsequent studies revealed that the American bias toward diagnosing Schizophrenia was incorrect, and that the Europeans made more accurate diagnoses. Today, Bipolar Disorder is diagnosed much more frequently than it was in the 1950s and 1960s, and Schizophrenia is diagnosed less frequently. In fact, there is good evidence that the incidence of Schizophrenia is dropping, at least in Northern European countries, and perhaps also in the United States and Canada.

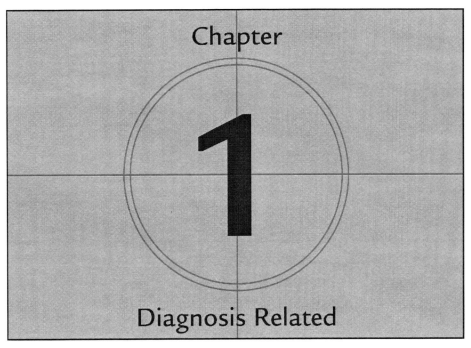

## Section Four - Anxiety Disorders

*"This is a neurotic's nightmare."*

Larry Lipton
(Woody Allen) in *Manhattan Murder Mystery*

*"[Seven people are dead] and I wish I were one of them."*

Aaron Altman
(Albert Brooks) in *Broadcast News*

*"The reason I was drinking, I was seeing all them things here that I had seen over there . . . Everyone trying to forget"*

Alvin Straight
(Richard Farnsworth) in *The Straight Story*

---

**Movie Clips:**

| | |
|---|---|
| *Midnight Run* .............. | Panic Attack |
| *Manhattan Murder Mystery* .... | Panic Attack, Agoraphobia |
| *Broadcast News* ............ | Performance Anxiety |
| *Four Weddings and a Funeral* ... | Performance Anxiety, Stage Fright and Shyness |
| *As Good as it Gets* .......... | Obsessive Compulsive Disorder |
| *The Straight Story* .......... | Posttraumatic Stress Disorder and Substance Abuse |

# Definitions

## Chapter 1- Diagnosis Related - Section Four

### Posttraumatic Stress Disorder

A. The person is exposed to a traumatic event in which both -
1) He or she experienced, witnessed, or was confronted with an event that threatened death or serious injury
2) The response included fear, horror, or helplessness

B. The traumatic event is persistently reexperienced in one or more ways -
1) Recurrent and intrusive distressing recollections including images, thoughts, or perceptions
2) Recurrent distressing dreams
3) Acting or feeling as if the event is recurring
4) Intense psychological distress at cues that symbolize the event
5) Physiological reactivity upon exposure to the cues

C. Persistent avoidance of stimuli associated with the trauma, and general numbing as indicated by at least three of the following -
1) Efforts to avoid thoughts, feelings, or conversations associated with the trauma
2) Efforts to avoid people, places, or activities that arouse recollections of the trauma
3) Inability to remember an important aspect of the trauma
4) Markedly diminished interest or participation in significant activities
5) Feelings of detachment or estrangement from others
6) Restricted range of affect (e.g., inability to show love)
7) Sense of foreshortened future

D. Persistent symptoms of increased arousal -
1) Difficulty falling or staying asleep
2) Irritability or outbursts of anger
3) Difficulty concentrating
4) Hyper-vigilance
5) Exaggerated startle response

E. Disorder causes significant distress or impaired functioning.

*(continued on page 37)*

# Criteria for Panic Attack

A discrete period of intense fear or discomfort, in which four or more of the following symptoms develop abruptly and reach a peak within ten minutes:

A. Palpitations, pounding heart, or rapid heartbeat
B. Sweating
C. Trembling or shaking
D. Sensations of shortness of breath or smothering
E. Feeling of choking
F. Chest pain or discomfort
G. Nausea or abdominal distress
H. Feeling dizzy, lightheaded, unsteady, or faint
I. De-realization (feelings of unreality) or de-personalization (being detached from oneself)
J. Fear of losing control or going crazy
K. Fear of dying
L. Paresthesias (numbness or tingling sensation)
M. Chills or hot flashes

# Agoraphobia

A. Anxiety about being in places or situations from which **escape might be difficult or embarrassing** or in which help might not be available in the event of having unexpected or situationally predisposed panic attack or panic-like symptoms. Fears often include being outside the home alone, being in a crowd or standing in a line, being on a bridge, or traveling in an airplane, bus, train or automobile.
B. The situation is avoided (travel is restricted, for example) or else endured with marked distress or with anxiety about having a panic attack, or require the presence of a companion.

# Panic Disorder

A. At least two (usually many more) unexpected Panic Attacks.
B. The Panic Attacks are not caused by a substance (e.g., caffeine or a medication) or a general medical condition.
C. The Panic Disorder is described as With Agoraphobia or Without Agoraphobia.

# Social Phobia

A. Marked and persistent fear of one or more **social or performance situations** in which the person is exposed to unfamiliar people or scrutiny by others. The individual fears that he or she will show anxiety or act in a way that is embarrassing or humiliating.

*(continued on page 38)*

B. Exposure to the situation provokes severe anxiety, often in the form of a panic attack.
C. The person knows the fear is excessive and unreasonable.
D. The situations are avoided or are endured with intense anxiety.
E. The avoidance, anxious anticipation or distress is severe and interferes with functioning.

Generalized Social Phobia involves fears of most social situations.

## Obsessive-Compulsive Disorder

A. Either Obsessions or Compulsions

***Obsessions are defined by (1) through (3) below***

1) Recurrent thoughts, images, or impulses (e.g., fear that the house will burn if the oven is not checked twelve times) that are intrusive and inappropriate, and induce anxiety or distress
2) These are not merely excessive worries about real-life problems
3) The person attempts to ignore, suppress, or neutralize the thoughts

***Compulsions are defined as (1) and (2) below***

1) Repetitive behaviors (e.g., hand washing, ordering, checking) or mental acts (e.g., counting, praying) that the person feels driven to perform in response to an obsession
2) The behaviors or mental acts are aimed at preventing or reducing distress or at preventing a dreaded event, even though they are not connected in a realistic way to the event or situation.

B. The person realizes that the obsessions or compulsions are unreasonable.
C. The obsessions or compulsions cause marked distress, consume **more than an hour a day**, or interfere with normal (work, academic or social) functioning.

# *Midnight Run*

| | |
|---|---|
| **Date of Movie:** | 1988 |
| **Actors in this scene:** | Robert De Niro as Jack Walsh |
| | Charles Grodin as Jonathan Mardukas |

**Timing on DVD:**

| | |
|---|---|
| 0:03:10 | Title |
| 0:22:27 | Start |
| 0:25:00 | End |

**Start of scene (VHS):** 0:19:17 after the title
A flight attendant helps them to their seats. Jack Walsh says, "That's fine, thanks."

**End of scene (VHS):** 0:21:50 after title
The scene inside the plane ends, and the sign for the train station announces their next mode of transportation.

**Duration of scene:** 2:33

---

**Summary of Movie:**
Jonathan Mardukas is an accountant who has been convicted of embezzlement, but who has eluded capture. Not only is the FBI tracking him down, but organized crime figures also pursue him, since he stole the mob's money. Walsh is a third party tracking him down, since he is a bounty hunter and will get paid by the bail bondsman. As Walsh brings Mardukas across country to turn him in, they are pursued both by the FBI and the mob, and their contradictory personalities (Walsh is crude and abrasive while Jonathan is clean cut and even-tempered) make this a buddy movie with a twist.

**Summary of scene:**
Jack Walsh brings Jonathan Mardukas onto a commercial airplane to fly him back to Los Angeles. Jonathan protests that he is unable to fly. Jack dismisses Jonathan's protestations and instead revels in the opportunity to fly first class with a better class of criminal. He jokes about the food in the first class section, and indicates that he plans to get some "surf and turf." Jonathan then has a Panic Attack - he is frightened, anxious, short of breath and hyperventilating, grunting, biting his thumb, and shouting that he is terrified and believes the plane will "go down." The captain of the plane kicks them off the plane, admonishing Jack Walsh for taking an unwilling prisoner on a commercial airline.

# *Midnight Run*: Insight Questions

For the sake of discussion, let us say that Jonathan has a Panic Attack in this scene. [In fact he faked the Panic Attack.] Have you ever had a Panic Attack (severe, sudden anxiety) or have you ever witnessed someone having one? What physical symptoms occurred during the attack?

Jonathan says that the plane will crash and they will die. People who have Panic Attacks usually fear that something horrible will happen. What are those fears – what do they fear will happen to them?

Jonathan did not want to fly on the airplane. People with Panic Disorder avoid situations in which they cannot escape easily. What are examples of those situations?

Jack tells Jonathan to calm down. Does it help you when someone tells you to calm down? Does it help when someone says that everything will be all right?

Jack ignored Jonathan's distress and instead made light of it. Is it helpful to ignore someone who acts strangely or who is highly anxious?

40        © 2004 Wellness Reproductions & Publishing 1.800.669.9208

# *Midnight Run*: Discussion Outline

**What symptoms of a Panic Attack does Jonathan Mardukas display?**

He exhibits . . .

- A discrete period of intense fear or discomfort
- Shortness of breath or smothering
- Fear of dying
- Fear of losing control or going crazy

He may have other symptoms. People with Panic Attacks are so overcome with emotions that they frequently fail to mention several symptoms. Clinicians should ask about each of the symptoms on the DSM IV list.

Panic Attacks vary from person to person. Some people experience lightheadedness, while others have a pounding heart and sweating.

## Is this Agoraphobia?

Please refer to the discussion in *Manhattan Murder Mystery*, page 43, about Agoraphobia. Those with Agoraphobia have a fear of being closed in and fear of places from which escape is difficult or embarrassing. Certainly, many people with Agoraphobia hate flying on airplanes, or they avoid the experience altogether.

Nonetheless, in some ways Jonathan does **not** seem to have Agoraphobia. Those with Agoraphobia fear being closed in and they dislike airplanes because they are unable to escape during the flight. They are trapped. I had one patient who insisted that her husband "stand guard" outside the little airplane lavatory, since she was terrified that it would lock closed, and she left it unlocked to assure that she would not be trapped in the airplane lavatory. As a result, she needed a guard. In this scene, in contrast, Jonathan Mardukas does not mention fear of being trapped. Instead he describes fear that the airplane will crash. Fear of crashing is quite normal, and is no more common among those with Agoraphobia (or Panic Disorder) than among the general public. This scene does not demonstrate Agoraphobia.

If Jack Walsh had realized that this was not Agoraphobia, he might have figured out that Jonathan Mardukas was fooling him. But then we would not have been able to enjoy the subsequent escapades and the great movie.

## In what ways is this scene consistent with Panic Disorder?

The Panic Attack is quite realistic. It has a sudden onset, which is accurate. He knows that being on an airplane will cause the attack; those with Panic Disorder and Agoraphobia know what situations trigger the attacks. The symptoms are severe to the point of being disabling, which is also characteristic of a Panic Attack. Panic Attacks are not merely anxiety or worry - they are significantly more distressing than that.

42

# Manhattan Murder Mystery

**Date of Movie:** 1993

**Actors in this scene:** Diane Keaton as Carol Lipton
Woody Allen as Larry Lipton

**Timing on DVD:**
| | |
|---|---|
| 0:00:34 | Title |
| 1:10:57 | Start |
| 1:13:09 | End |

**Start of scene (VHS):** 1:10:23 after the title
Carol and Larry press the button to call the elevator.

**End of scene (VHS):** 1:12:3
The lights go out on the elevator.

**Duration of scene:** 2:12

**Summary of Movie:**
Carol and Larry are a married couple living in an apartment building in New York. Another couple lives in the same apartment building, and the wife disappears. Carol and Larry suspect that the husband has murdered the wife, but the police are uninterested in the case. Carol, Larry and their friends themselves investigate the possible crime, although lack of a body hinders their progress.

**Summary of Scene:**
Carol and Larry have just snooped around the apartment of the possible killer, and they are leaving the apartment furtively. Larry is leery about the whole enterprise and does not believe they should be investigating. Larry and Carol argue as they board the elevator. The elevator stops unexpectedly between floors and they are trapped. Larry gets panicky - he is fearful, he moves his hands excitedly, he worries, his voice rises, he is tense, and he is short of breath. He describes himself as a world-renown claustrophobic. Carol tells him to relax and not to worry, and she assures him that someone will help. Larry tries to calm himself by imagining that he is a stallion running over fields in an open meadow, with a cool breeze whistling through his hair. Carol tells him to "shut up and calm down" as he gets more frantic and fears the worst. As the tension rises, they push open the top of the elevator car only to reveal a dead body, and the lights on the elevator go out. As the scene ends, Larry says, "This is a neurotic's nightmare."

# *Manhattan Murder Mystery*: Insight Questions

As soon as the elevator got stuck, Larry panicked. Have you ever experienced "instant panic?" What triggered it?

When Carol told Larry to calm down, she sounded irritated with him. Describe a situation in which someone was irritated with you for being fearful. On the other hand, are you weary of people who are frequently in crisis and frequently upset?

Larry visualized being a stallion running across fields. List three visualizations (mental images) that help you handle stress.

Larry called himself a world-renowned neurotic. Which neurotic tendencies do you battle . . . what are your triggers for anxiety?

Three things happened: the elevator stuck, the dead body appeared, and the lights went out. What are two or three of your greatest fears?

# *Manhattan Murder Mystery*: Discussion Outline

### How rapidly did Larry's symptoms develop?

They developed within a matter of seconds. People who have Panic Disorder with or without Agoraphobia develop frequent Panic Attacks, and these attacks characteristically have a nearly instantaneous onset. The rapidity of onset is a key feature of the disorder, and it distinguishes Panic Disorder from other types of anxiety.

"Garden variety" anxiety builds gradually - as the fearful situation develops or unfolds, the anxiety gradually builds to a crescendo. However, those with true Panic Attacks have a very rapid onset of extremely disabling anxiety.

### Which symptoms of a Panic Attack did Larry experience?

In my office, I inquire about all of the symptoms mentioned in the Diagnostic and Statistical Manual, 4th Edition (DSM IV). During the course of treatment, together we monitor these symptoms – which ones improve and which do not.

He had a discrete period of intense fear or discomfort (part of the definition of the disorder) plus these symptoms:

- Sweating
- Sensations of shortness of breath or smothering
- Fear of losing control or becoming insane
- Fear of dying
- Feeling dizzy or faint
- Chills or hot flashes

### How intense are his symptoms?

They are crippling. Those with Panic Attacks often find it difficult to convince other people how severe the symptoms are. They get particularly frustrated when other people minimize their suffering, and suggest that they should just "ignore" the symptoms, since it is "just anxiety." The symptoms are so severe that people believe that they are dying or "going crazy."

*(continued on page 46)*

45

## How successful is Carol at calming Larry?

She fails miserably. She tells him to calm down, and says that everything will be all right. Such platitudes do not help those with Panic Attacks. She does not appreciate the intensity of his symptoms. Her reaction may reflect that she is weary of dealing with Larry's Panic Attacks.

Similarly, Larry's attempts at self-help are ineffective. Presumably, he has either seen a therapist or read a self-help book, since he attempts to visualize a calming scene. Frequently, such visualization, especially if it is more of an intellectual exercise than one that is practiced, is useless in the midst of a full-blown Panic Attack.

## How does the presence of Panic Disorder or Agoraphobia affect a marriage?

Often, the person with Panic Attacks becomes dependent on the other person for shopping, driving, and for emotional reassurance. The marriage becomes intense, and caretaking is commonplace. When the disorder is treated, the marriage may have to change or dissolve.

## How do you treat Panic Disorder?

Psychological treatments address both Panic Attacks and Agoraphobia. Patients are taught calming techniques, such as slow breathing (partly to combat the hyperventilation), relaxation, mental imaging, and related techniques. Cognitive therapy addresses the negative self-talk involving catastrophic thinking, fears of death, dependency, and low esteem. Behavioral approaches emphasize the importance of facing the feared situations and not avoiding them; one suggestion is to make a list of feared situations, and spend about an hour each day in the situation (until the person is bored). In addition, patients must identify triggers for attacks, which could include general stress, becoming overly tired, being premenstrual, using marijuana, cocaine or alcohol, or not sleeping enough.

Books (bibliotherapy) are helpful. Self-help books allow people to realize that they are not alone, that they will not die, and that they can cope actively rather than becoming a passive victim to the disorder.

Medicine is very effective. Antidepressants (both SSRIs and tricyclics) are helpful, although they take a few weeks to work, they have side effects, and they may not be totally effective. Benzodiazepines such as Xanax (alprazolam) and Klonopin (clonazepam) are very effective and work rapidly, but they have addictive potential.

The disorder is very treatable. Patients can learn to manage the disorder, which may be episodic throughout their lives, and to avoid unnecessary trips to the Emergency Room and unnecessary medical tests.

# Broadcast News (1)

**Date of Movie:** 1987

**Actors in this scene:** Albert Brooks as Aaron Altman

**Timing on DVD:**
| | |
|---|---|
| 0:05:07 | Title |
| 1:22:58 | Start |
| 1:25:32 | End |

**Start of scene (VHS):** 1:17:52 after the title
Cut from the party attended by Tom Grunick (played by William Hurt) and Jane Craig (played by Holly Hunter) to the newsroom, where Aaron Altman sits in the Anchor Chair.

**End of scene (VHS):** 1:20:26 after title
"I wish I were one of them," which ends the newsroom scene.

**Duration of scene:** 2:34

**Summary of Movie:**
This drama chronicles the rise of a telegenic though uninformed newscaster, Tom Grunick, at the expense of his hard working, intelligent, knowledgeable yet uncompromising mentor, Jane Craig, as well as the funny, sad, under-appreciated writer, Aaron Altman.

**Summary of Scene:**
Because the other anchors are unavailable, Aaron Altman gets his chance to anchor a late-breaking story on the local television newscast. He preps himself with all the tips suggested by Tom, and he reads the script from behind the news desk. He breaks into a world-class sweat that becomes more visible as time progresses. His shirt becomes stained and his face drips. The staff's attempts to help him (clean shirt, hair dryer) only make things worse, as they jiggle the set and as his discomfort reaches a climax. He ends his stint by commenting that seven people are dead (on air) and "I wish I were one of them" (off air).

# Broadcast News (1): Insight Questions

In what situation did you sweat excessively or have a massive physical reaction to stress? Why did that particular situation cause the problem?

At the end of the scene Aaron wishes he were dead. In what situations have you felt that way, and what is your perspective now?

Have you ever had an experience of finally getting an opportunity to do something, and then you flopped, or the experience was a big disappointment? How do you understand it now?

In this scene the workers at the television studio help Aaron, and they give him encouragement. Amongst themselves they acknowledge how much he sweats, but they do not tell Aaron. What does it feel like when your friends do not tell you to your face how badly you know you are doing?

Imagine someone who feels very anxious in social situations. What problems or complications might that person experience in the long run from having that difficulty?

# *Broadcast News (1)*: Discussion Outline

### How does Aaron show his anxiety?

Sweating is a predominant symptom. He smacks his lips, perhaps in an attempt to deal with the perspiration. He may be trembling.

### What labels are used for this situation?

Social Phobia, Social Anxiety [Disease] and Performance Anxiety are labels often used to describe this situation. Performance Anxiety is a commonly used term that is not listed in DSM IV as a disorder, but is used to describe situations in which people get anxious when they are supposed to perform (often in public). Social Phobia is the official DSM IV diagnostic term, which some people would like to replace with the more descriptive term Social Anxiety Disorder.

### At what point does anxiety in social situations become an illness?

Social Phobia is considered a disorder, and not just a normal reaction to stress, when the fear is "excessive and unreasonable," and "interferes with functioning." This particular scene may not be indicative of a disorder if anxiety does not otherwise interfere with his functioning. However, if Aaron got severely anxious or had a panic attack every time he tried to speak in public (in small group settings or in meetings) then he would be more likely diagnosed as having a disorder.

Those with Social Phobia (or Social Anxiety) often avoid school to avoid speaking in class, quit jobs rather than speak in public, or use drugs or alcohol rather than face anxiety in social situations. Their disorder interferes with their functioning.

### How does Aaron Altman feel after this episode?

Often, people with Social Phobia feel humiliated, experience low self-esteem, and feel powerless and worthless. Not surprisingly, those with Social Phobia often also experience depression. They sometimes develop relationships with people who take care of them, but who do not treat them as mature adults. They then feel more childlike.

People with Social Phobia often respond well to treatment with medicine (especially medicine that affects serotonin, such as fluoxetine, sertraline, and other SSRI's). In addition, psychotherapy is crucial. Behaviorally oriented treatment focuses on the need to practice facing the feared situations. Cognitive therapy helps deal with the fear of failure, as well as with negative self-talk. It teaches people to combat negative statements such as "I'm stupid and weak" and "the anxiety will kill me."

*(continued on page 50)*

## Could you elaborate on cognitive-behavioral therapy?

Using cognitive therapy, Aaron will explicitly state his **automatic negative thoughts** (cognitions). These will include such statements as:

- I am a failure
- I will die if I go on the air again

After elaborating the common automatic negative thoughts, the cognitive therapist will get Aaron to respond to those globally negative statements with more **realistic appraisals** of the situation. Aaron may reply to those two negative statements above with statements such as the following:

- I sweat a lot, but did not fail in my assignment
- I did not perform as well as the other anchors, but this is the first time that I had the opportunity
- Even if I am not a good anchor, I have other talents
- I got anxious but did not come close to dying
- I can practice public speaking and get medical help if I plan to anchor in the future
- This was not a catastrophe; it was a setback

The behavioral aspect of the treatment involves "getting on the horse after falling off." He must practice public speaking, work on his mannerisms, and not avoid the situation (i.e., not give in to the phobia). In addition, the behavioral treatment may include relaxation exercises and the use of relaxing images to minimize distress.

## How do friends, acquaintances, and family members treat the person with the illness?

At first, they may laugh, as they did in this scene (and thus reinforce the humiliation). Once they know a bit more, they may encourage the person to face the feared situation, but in the process may minimize the intensity of the discomfort that the person with Social Phobia experiences. Others may become codependent, and be so "helpful" to the person with the disorder that he or she is shielded from ever having to face the situations and the symptoms. The optimal response is to acknowledge the severity of the disorder, and, at the same time, encourage professional help and gradual orientation to facing social situations once the individual starts therapy.

## Four Weddings and a Funeral

**Date of Movie:** 1994

**Actors in this scene:**
Rowan Atkinson as Father Gerald
Sophie Thompson as Lydia Hibbott
David Haig as Bernard Delaney

**Timing on DVD:**
| | |
|---|---|
| 0:00:36 | Title |
| 0:36:54 | Start |
| 0:41:06 | End |

**Start of scene (VHS):** 0:36:18 after the title
Bridesmaid grabs her red wig as she enters the church for a wedding.   .

**End of scene (VHS):** 0:40:30
One wedding guest shouts, "Bravo!" as the music starts, the wedding ceremony ends, the couple kisses, and the scene inside the church ends

**Duration of scene:** 4:12

---

**Summary of Movie:**
A subtle British comedy focuses on a group of friends and their search for sustainable relationships and true love. Each ceremony illuminates another aspect of the struggle.

**Summary of Scene:**
Father Gerald performs his first wedding ceremony in a glorious high church, and stumbles over several words, creating delightful double entendres, including "your awful wedded wife" and "the Father, Son, and Holy Spigot." He sweats and smacks his lips. His anxiety is contagious. All eyes are upon him, as the dignified parents look down their noses at his bumbling, while the younger generation laughs and ridicules him.

# *Four Weddings and a Funeral*: Insight Questions

Have you ever known anyone who suffered extreme anxiety whenever he or she spoke in public? Did you know anyone in school who skipped school whenever she or he had to speak in front of the class?

Among those who fear public speaking, what reaction do they fear they will get from others?

How does an experience similar to the one in the movie scene affect someone's self esteem?

Imagine that someone is aware that he or she gets extremely nervous whenever public speaking is required. How do you think that person deals with requests to speak in public, such as reciting a poem in English class or speaking in group meetings at work?

How can someone deal with extreme fear of public speaking?

# *Four Weddings and a Funeral*: Discussion Outline

## What heightens the expectations and the sense of drama?

- Weddings always are important. This is the biggest day in the life of a woman (according to legend).
- The church is monstrous and dignified - high church at its grandest.
- The guests look especially well-dressed. This is not a casual affair.
- Whispered talk reveals that this is the first service that Gerald has performed. This is his big day too.
- Father Gerald is a friend of the family. He does not want to let them down.
- The music is especially grand and glorious.

All of these elements contribute to the building of expectations. These expectations heighten the possibility of performance anxiety.

## Father Gerald makes several verbal mishaps. Does this bother him?

Yes, his discomfort is clear. He sweats, and he licks his lips to deal with the perspiration. He hesitates for a long time before pronouncing someone's middle name, evidently terrified that he will once again mispronounce that name. He triumphantly nods to indicate his pleasure at getting it right (finally). At the end of the ceremony he lets out a sigh and displays great relief.

## How does the congregation heighten his misery?

The father of the bride glares over his reading glasses, with a contemptuous and overbearing demeanor. The younger guests snicker, giggle, and barely contain raucous laughter. A sarcastic "bravo" reverberates when the ceremony ends.

## Is this scene consistent with Social Phobia?

Yes, all of the elements are in place. First, we have a performance situation. Second, we have the hapless performer who wilts under scrutiny. Third, we have the public response.

This scene is quite similar to the one in *Broadcast News*, page 47. If someone experiences overwhelming anxiety in just one venue, then we do not label it with a diagnosis. However, if it is a pattern of overwhelming anxiety in repeated situations of social performance, then we consider the diagnosis of Social Phobia. If such episodes only occur in a few specific and predictable venues, such as public speaking, then we consider the **specific type** of Social Phobia, whereas we consider the **generalized type** if the pattern occurs in widespread situations.

*(continued on page 54)*

53

## Does this really happen?

Those with Social Phobia do not get themselves into situations such as these. They avoid public speaking, especially situations as charged as this one. Furthermore, their public performances, when they do happen, are usually marked by modest outward anxiety, but with marked inward turmoil. This scene does not depict what happens to those with Social Phobia, but does depict what they **fear** will occur.

# *As Good As It Gets*

| | |
|---|---|
| **Date of Movie:** | 1998 |
| **Actors in this scene:** | Jack Nicholson as Melvin Udall<br>Helen Hunt as Carol Connelly |
| **Timing on DVD:** | 0:01:47    Title<br>0:10:07    Start<br>0:14:31    End |
| **Start of scene (VHS):** | 0:08:18 after the title<br>Melvin Udall walks out of an apartment building, down the steps, and onto the sidewalk. |
| **End of scene (VHS):** | 0:12:42 after the title<br>Carol arises from the table and says, "Okay, I'll get your order." |
| **Duration of scene:** | 4:24 |

---

**Summary of Movie:**
Hostile, financially successful, obsessive-compulsive writer learns to show compassion after coming to terms with some of his own failings. He overcomes his hostility and helps a beleaguered and beaten up gay man (played by Greg Kinnear) and Carol, a struggling mother / waitress.

**Summary of Scene:**
Melvin leaves his apartment, walks on the sidewalk in such a way that he avoids cracks and avoids touching other people, and he then arrives at the restaurant that he visits every day. He is upset that others are sitting at his usual table. He makes an anti-Semitic remark to drive the other customers away. He lays out his sterile plasticware in a ritualistic fashion. He makes a cruel statement about death, and in the process he alienates Carol, the only waitress who tolerates him.

## As Good As It Gets: Insight Questions

Have you ever known someone with Obsessive-Compulsive Disorder (OCD)? If so, how did you become aware of the symptoms or the disorder?

If you have known someone with OCD, what symptoms did that person have? If you have not known anyone with OCD, what symptoms of that illness are you aware of?

Do you think that someone with OCD is aware that his or her obsessions or compulsions are silly, unfounded or ridiculous? Why or why not?

Considering those with OCD who live with others, what impact do you think their symptoms have on family members?

How much time do you imagine someone with OCD spends each day concerned with the symptoms of the disorder?

# As Good As It Gets: Discussion Outline

Note: The reader is referred to scene of *As Good As It Gets* in chapter 3, page 151, for additional discussion of OCD.

## What compulsions does Melvin exhibit?

- He avoids stepping on cracks in the pavement
- He avoids touching people
- He brings his own sterile eating utensils
- He aligns his utensils in a pre-determined manner
- He insists on sitting in his usual location

## How are obsessions related to these compulsions?

Obsessions are thoughts, and compulsions are actions. Most professionals believe that obsessions trigger compulsions. In this scene, they would hypothesize that . . .

- He avoids cracks, because he believes that stepping on a crack may bring bad luck, such as causing his mother to break her back.
- He avoids touching people because he is obsessed with germs, and thinks that he will be exposed to contagion if he touches people.
- He brings his own utensils because he can assure that they do not carry germs.
- People with Obsessive-Compulsive Disorder do not know why they desire symmetry, but sometimes they explain that if everything is symmetrical, then they feel less anxious since the world is now more orderly and proper.

## Besides Melvin's compulsions, what are common symptoms of OCD?

*Checking* compulsions are common. People with OCD check . . .
- Locks on doors
- Stoves
- Whether the car motor is turned off (one patient laid on the hood of the car to feel vibrations)
- To see if they have hit someone with the car. They repeatedly look in the rear view mirror and circle the block to assure that no one is injured. One patient circled blocks repeatedly, then called the police to confess in advance to any hit and run accidents.

*Symmetry* plays out in many ways. People with OCD . . .
- Assure that the bed is made exactly right
- Align shoes properly
- Store clothes exactly right
- Balance one thought or statement with another one

*(continued on page 58)*

*Counting* is pervasive. People with OCD count . . .

- Tiles in ceilings
- Steps
- Phrases or statements (e.g., saying eight "Hail Mary's" whenever a certain cue occurs.)

*Hoarding* (this is the most difficult to extinguish) may involve . . .

- Newspapers, for fear of missing an important item, leading to houses filled with papers and trash. Local government may have to intervene.
- Trinkets and other expendable belongings.

## Does Melvin have Obsessive-Compulsive Disorder?

The scene does not convey enough information to be sure. He certainly seems to have compulsions (Criterion A, page 38). These compulsions interfere with normal social functioning (Criterion C). We do not know whether he realizes that the compulsions are unreasonable. Later in the movie he tells Carol that he sees a psychiatrist in order to deal with his problem, and even reluctantly started taking medicine. He later attempts to break his compulsion to avoid walking on cracks. Evidence from late in the movie suggests that he also meets Criterion B of OCD, thus fulfilling all of the necessary criteria to make the diagnosis.

## Why is Criterion B so important (realization that the obsessions and compulsions are unreasonable)?

If the individual believes that the obsession is reasonable, then he is out of touch with reality, and the symptom would be labeled as a delusion rather than an obsession. People with delusions are more likely to have a diagnosis of Schizophrenia than Obsessive-Compulsive Disorder.

The treatment implications are enormous. Those with OCD can be induced to fight their symptoms, and will engage in behaviorally oriented therapy to deal with it. Response prevention (which is also used for Agoraphobia and Social Phobia) is the centerpiece of the therapy. Medicine (SSRI's) is also crucial to the treatment of OCD.

Treatment of delusions is vastly different. First, an accurate diagnosis must be made, and it may be Schizophrenia or a related disorder. Since delusions are defined as false, fixed beliefs, it is nearly impossible to convince a delusional person to fight the delusion. That person believes the delusion is true, so why fight it? The medicine is different too. Antipsychotic medicine is the best treatment, whereas SSRI's are much less helpful.

## Melvin is cruel. Are people with the diagnosis of Obsessive Compulsive Disorder cruel?

Studies have verified that close friends and families of those with OCD experience significant distress. The individual with OCD often insists, as Melvin did in this scene, that others accommodate to his illness. In this scene, Melvin acts horribly to others in his quest to appease his compulsions.

## Does Melvin realize how he comes across?

Melvin seems unaware of his effect on others. He seems concerned only with himself, and he makes a cruel comment to Carol, who is one of the only people on the planet that he cares for. When he makes the comment, he does not appreciate its impact. He believes that he is merely making a statement of fact.

The psychoanalytically inclined clinicians would recognize his psychological defense as "isolation of affect." That is, he is oblivious to his effect on others, and to his cruelty. All of his affect — his feelings — are wrapped up in his obsessions and compulsions.

Character development makes this a great movie. Melvin starts to overcome his isolation of affect. He becomes better able to recognize his feelings, to recognize the impact of his behavior on others, to care about others, and to strive to become a better person.

# The Straight Story

| | |
|---|---|
| **Date of Movie:** | 1999 |
| **Actors in this scene:** | Richard Farnsworth as Richard Straight<br>Wiley Harker as Verlyn Heller |
| **Timing on DVD:** | 0:00:42     Title<br>1:15:38     Start<br>1:21:39     End |
| **Start of scene (VHS):** | 1:14:55 after the title<br>The beginning of the scene: two old men drinking (milk and beer) at a bar. |
| **End of scene (VHS):** | 1:20:56 after the title<br>End of bar scene |
| **Duration of scene:** | 6:01 |

**Summary of Movie:**
Alvin Straight is a 73-year-old man who lives in western Iowa. He decides to visit his ill brother, Lyle, from whom he has been estranged for ten years, in Mount Zion, Wisconsin. He drives a John Deere lawnmower 300 miles over the course of five weeks, across the Iowa and Wisconsin landscape. His moving encounters with strangers reflect on the vitality and frailty of our connections with our loved ones, the effects of time and age, remembering and forgetting.

**Summary of Scene:**
Alvin no longer drinks alcohol because he overindulged and became "mean." "The reason I was drinking, I was seeing all them things here that I had seen over there." "Everyone trying to forget . . . " He recounts inadvertently killing his friend during World War II, and keeping it a secret.

Verlyn remembers his buddies in World War II being burned to death while eating their first hot meal in eleven days. "That's one thing I can't shake loose. All my buddies' faces are still young."

## *The Straight Story*: Insight Questions

Have you ever talked to someone about his or her war experiences? Did he or she speak with emotion?

How have people described their dreams and nightmares of their traumatic memories? Have you ever seen someone startle when confronted with someone or something that reminded him or her of a traumatic event?

Have you known anyone who drank alcohol to help forget past experiences? Did that person drink excessively?

Do you think it was helpful for Verlyn and Alvin to discuss their wartime memories? Why or why not?

Why do you think that these two men spoke openly to each other? What conditions make it possible for you to discuss painful memories?

# *The Straight Story*: Discussion Outline

## What is Posttraumatic Stress Disorder?

It is the reexperiencing of an extremely traumatic event, as well as increased arousal (insomnia, agitation, anger, hypervigilance) and avoidance of anything that brings to mind the previous trauma. Traumatic events include military combat, violent personal assault (including abuse and rape), torture, disasters, automobile accidents and others.

## Do they meet the threshold for Criterion A (exposure to traumatic event)?

Yes. They experienced and witnessed death, in situations in which they were horrified, helpless and scared.

## Do they reexperience the event (Criterion B)?

They both seem to "persistently reexperience their trauma," since Alvin says that he was "seeing them things over here that I had seen over there." Verlyn can not "shake loose" the faces of his buddies. They seem to act as if the events are recurring, since we hear war noises when they speak of their traumas. They both recall, decades later, the most intimate details: how their buddies looked and where they were from ("A little fella. A Polish boy from Milwaukee.").

This scene also captures the idiosyncratic nature of some of those memories. Alvin remembers the faces, preserved as if they had not aged, while Verlyn recalls the insignia on the airplane.

## Do they avoid stimuli associated with the traumatic events, and do they experience numbing?

The major thrust of the scene is that Alvin used alcohol to numb his pain, while Verlyn continues to numb his pain with beer. Alvin comments on "everyone trying to forget." He kept secret for decades the fact that he shot his friend. A clinician would probe for other signs that Alvin and Verlyn avoid stimuli related to their memories. They seem to meet Criterion C.

This scene depicts the connection between PTSD and alcoholism: many people abuse alcohol to dull their feelings, and to avoid the painful memories. The alcohol in turn leads to its own problems - alcoholism, mood disorder and others. Those with PTSD suffer from alcohol and drug related problems more than do others in the general population.

They sit side-by-side, but avoid eye contact as they stare straight ahead and talk to the mirror or the wall. Some would say that stoical Midwestern men always speak to each other in that manner.

In contrast to their staring ahead as they speak, their conversation overcomes some of the usual barriers to talking. They spend time together, stay sober and coherent, and share intimate details of their most painful memories.

*(continued on page 62)*

In the chapter on grief (see the discussion about *Truly Madly Deeply*, page 127, and the one about *Saving Private Ryan*, page 119), I contend that it is sometimes useful to share one's own memories as an aid to establishing the empathic bond. In this scene in *The Straight Story* these men each share a painful memory, perhaps aided by knowing that the other man is empathic, as witnessed by his willingness to open up. One man's openness enabled the other to share his own memory.

## Do they continue to show signs of increased arousal?

The scene from *The Fisher King*, page 109, shows increased arousal. A clinical interview may reveal more than this scene shows. However, Alvin acknowledges that he became "mean" on a regular basis, and we assume that he used alcohol to dampen his strong physiologic responses to his memories. We have not been able to evaluate their anger, hypervigilance, concentration, sleep or startle response. They may meet Criterion D.

## Are they impaired or distressed by the symptoms?

We do not know if they are significantly impaired by these symptoms, or have significant distress. Their faces and body language show us that they continue to be affected by these experiences: they seem despondent, moody, and weary. I think I detected tears, 50 years later. We do not know if they meet Criterion E.

## How long does PTSD last?

As this scene illustrates (the movie is based on a true story), the symptoms of PTSD can last a lifetime. People with PTSD can benefit from therapy with a person skilled in treating those with PTSD.

In the last few years, many men and women who fought in World War II spoke about their experiences for the first time. The books by Stephen Ambrose (D-Day, Band of Brothers, and Citizen Soldiers), Tom Brokaw (The Greatest Generation) and James Bradley (Flags of Our Father) as well as the movie *Saving Private Ryan* have been very popular, and their popularity has been fueled by that generation's determination finally to deal with its past.

## What do you make of these old men?

We do a disservice to our elders if we assume that they are sweet old things without a lifetime of stored emotions. I recall being shocked when a 78-year-old patient described sexual orgies in the 1930s; I had not wanted to think about such behavior in people the age of my parents and grandparents. The men in this scene are fully developed characters - they are not stereotypes.

The acting is understated and powerful. These actors are entirely believable as they choke back tears and struggle with long-ago hurts.

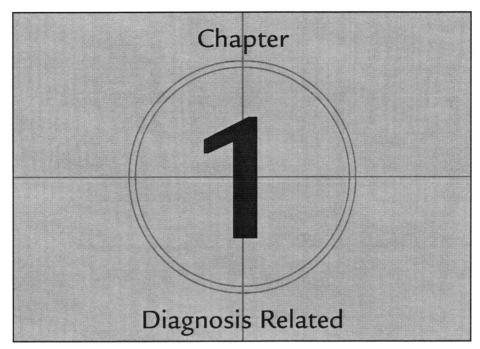

# Section Five - Substance Abuse and Dependence

*"Turn the hot light off and the cool light on."*

Jasper
(Dominic West) in *28 Days*

**Movie Clips:**

*28 Days* . . . . . . . . . . . . . . . . . Alcohol and Drug Dependence; Enabling
*Traffic* . . . . . . . . . . . . . . . . . . . Drug Dependence, Drugs and the Family
*Clean and Sober* . . . . . . . . . . . . A Sober Life
*Affliction* . . . . . . . . . . . . . . . . . Alcohol Dependence; Adult Child of Alcoholic

# Definitions

## Chapter 1- Diagnosis Related - Section Five

### Substance Abuse

A maladaptive pattern of substance use with repeated negative consequences related to the use of substances. The adverse consequences include:
  A. Failure to meet obligations at work, home or school
  B. Using substance in unsafe situations such as driving automobiles
  C. Legal problems
  D. Social problems such as arguments and fights

### Substance Dependence

A maladaptive pattern of substance use, leading to clinically significant impairment or distress, with **three or more** of the following:
  A. Tolerance for markedly increased amounts of the substance
  B. Withdrawal symptoms
  C. Using larger amounts over a longer period of time than was intended
  D. Persistent desire or unsuccessful efforts to cut down, or control, use of the substance
  E. A great deal of time is spent in activities necessary to obtain the substance, use the substance, or recover from its effects
  F. Important social, occupational, or recreational activities are given up, or reduced, because of substance abuse
  G. The substance is used despite the problems that its use causes

# 28 Days

| | |
|---|---|
| **Date of Movie:** | 2000 |
| **Actors in this scene:** | Sandra Bullock as Gwen Cummings<br>Dominic West as Jasper |
| **Timing on DVD:** | 0:00:46　Title<br>0:45:45　Start<br>0:48:40　End |
| **Start of scene (VHS):** | 0:44:58 after the title<br>A man and a woman are in a boat on a lake. |
| **End of scene (VHS):** | 0:47:53 after the title<br>The scene in the boat ends. |
| **Duration of scene:** | 2:55 |

**Summary of Movie:**
A successful New York journalist ruins her sister's wedding during a drunken binge. After picking up a DUI (Driving Under the Influence of alcohol), she goes to an alcohol and drug treatment center, where she confronts her addiction and her feelings.

**Summary of Scene:**
Jasper visits Gwen at the treatment center and takes her out on the lake in a boat. He insists that there is nothing wrong with her ("don't let them tell you there is something wrong with you"), and that she is "surrounded by a bunch of sober freaks." Gwen tells him that she has difficulties, and he undermines that belief by rationalizing it ("you just did a rot – it happens to everyone"), and by denying that she can be happy without drugs and alcohol ("that's a crock of shit"). He even supports the use of alcohol as the universal healer, stating that some people deal with life's pain "by getting wasted."

Jasper proposes marriage to Gwen. He has the engagement ring embedded in the bread (which she doesn't want to eat) and he brings champagne in a thermos. Gwen is astounded that he would propose marriage to her during her treatment, and she pours out the champagne. He expresses irritation and amazement that she does not see this as a romantic moment, and she retorts that she is not taking her addiction and recovery as lightly as he is.

# *28 Days*: Insight Questions

Jasper tells Gwen that she does not have a problem. Have you noticed people telling alcoholics or addicts that they do not have a problem?

Jasper brings champagne for Gwen to drink, even though she is alcoholic. What message is he giving, and what is he trying to accomplish?

Jasper tells her that she is surrounded by "a bunch of sober freaks." How does that statement undermine her treatment?

Jasper insists that Gwen break the bread and eat it even though she does not like bread. Similarly, he does not listen to her when she says that she has a serious problem with alcohol. What does that say about his level of denial and his empathy for her?

Jasper says that alcohol helps people deal with pain and unhappiness, and he romanticizes it when he talks about "turning the hot light off and the cool light on." In what ways have you noticed that some people romanticize or justify drinking alcohol to excess?

# *28 Days*: Discussion Outline

**What is the first of the twelve steps of Alcoholic Anonymous?**

"We admitted we were powerless over alcohol --- that our lives had become unmanageable."

**How does Gwen address that step?**

She mentions that she attends a rehabilitation clinic, implying that she needs help. She gets progressively more direct, as she states that, "I would like a life." She discards the thermos filled with champagne, literally throwing away a substance she cannot handle, and symbolically discarding a life that is unmanageable. She says that she is "not taking this as lightly as [she] used to." She continues by saying, "Maybe there is something wrong with me . . . I think they're right." She says that she can be happy without drinking and drugging. She ends the scene stating, "I don't feel fine . . . I'm such a mess."

Gwen changed. When she began treatment she believed that she could handle the chemicals, and now she knows that she cannot. She embraced the first step, and we, the viewers, realize that she has a chance for recovery.

**How does Jasper undermine her recovery?**

In numerous ways he tells Gwen that she is fine, and that she does not need a sober life. He states that her antics do not indicate a problem, and that the behaviors that got her in trouble "happen to everyone." He says that pain is the "human condition," and is not caused by drugs. His bringing champagne is his most blatant attempt to ruin her sobriety.

He goes further when he says, "That's a crock of shit," in response to her comment that one can be both happy and sober. He extols the medicinal virtues of alcohol and drugs, and states that "getting wasted" is an excellent way to deal with life's pain. He thus rationalizes the behavior.

He also seduces her to drink and drug, when his voice changes and he softly says that the drugs "turn the hot light off and the cool light on." In other words, drugs enhance life, and do not destroy life.

Splitting describes the phenomenon when the patient or client is split from the staff, or when staff members are divided and antagonistic to one another. In this scene Jasper says many things that serve to split Gwen from her treatment team. What did you notice in this respect?

▪ He refers to the people at the facility as "a bunch of sober freaks." That statement serves to cast aspersions on those who are sober, including many staff members.

*(continued on page 68)*

- She says that she is unhappy, and Jasper insists that she is unhappy because they are apart (which is necessitated by her being in treatment), whereas Gwen tries to convince him that she is unhappy because of the effects of alcohol. Thus, Jasper implies that her attempts to get treatment cause her unhappiness.
- When Gwen says that she "would like a life," Jasper says, " . . . that's what I thought I was offering." Jasper implies that she needs his love and not the efforts of the therapists.
- He thinks she needs a ring and champagne, and she thinks she needs treatment and sobriety instead. She pours out the champagne, symbolically pouring out her former lifestyle.
- When she says, "Maybe there is something wrong with me," he says that the therapists are incorrect in that assessment.

## Another method to undermine treatment is to glamorize the use of chemicals. How does Jasper use this technique?

- He pours her champagne in a romantic setting
- He praises the medicinal values of alcohol. He states, it "minimizes the pain"
- He mentions its seductive value in turning feelings hot or cold as desired
- He says that getting married in a pub would be "a good story"

## Jasper directly undermines Gwen's recovery. In what other ways does he undermine her?

His entire personality reeks of someone who cares more for himself than for others. At the outset he insists that she have bread even though she does not want it. He states that his marriage proposal has nothing to do with her being at a rehab center. He does not grasp that this treatment is very important for her. He just sees her being at the clinic as a bump in the road. Getting married in a pub "would make a good story." He prefers a good story to a healthy start to a marriage. He states that he is offering a life, and in a curious way is saying that he is in charge and that she is just along for the ride. He does not speak about a joining of two people and respect for each other, but instead he offers his own conception of a marriage. He is irritated when she disposes of the champagne, saying, "This is so not how I saw this whole thing playing out." In other words, he had his preconceived ideas of their relationship, and was so self-centered that he could only imagine her agreeing to his wishes.

In the future, if Gwen were to stay with Jasper, whether Gwen is sober or drinking, Jasper will always listen to himself first, and will not attend to Gwen's emotional needs. Her sobriety threatens him.

## How real to life is this scene?

I find the movie to be mediocre, and the scene to be heavy-handed. In my experience, those who jeopardize someone's sobriety do so in subtler ways than Jasper employs. Those who undermine treatment make belittling comments about the other patients, pointing out that the others seem so much sicker that the identified patient. Then they might question some of the spiritual aspects of the program. They might recall a funny drinking episode. But these undermining comments will be interspersed with superficially supportive comments.

# *Traffic*

| | |
|---|---|
| **Date of Movie:** | 2000 |
| **Actors in this scene:** | Michael Douglas as Robert Hudson Wakefield<br>Amy Irving as Barbara Wakefield<br>Erika Christensen as Caroline Wakefield |
| **Timing on DVD:** | 0:00:15    Title<br>0:41:29    Start<br>0:45:33    End |
| **Start of scene (VHS):** | 0:41:14 after the title<br>A seated girl is visible behind a windowed door at the start of the scene. A counselor asks, "How old are you?" |
| **End of scene (VHS):** | 0:45:18 after the title<br>Barbara says, "Six months." Robert stares, standing and exasperated. The scene ends. |
| **Duration of scene:** | 4:04 |

**Summary of Movie:**

This powerful, superbly conceived movie, delivers its punch without becoming preachy. The complex plot revolves around several barely connected story strands. We follow the story of two Mexican drug enforcement agents, two American DEA agents, a mid-level importer of drugs, a high-level drug czar and his loving / abetting wife, an American federal judge who is appointed national drug czar, the judge's addicted daughter, and the corrupt Mexican general who attacks the drug cartel.

**Summary of Scene:**

Caroline, the 16-year-old daughter of the recently appointed drug czar, is questioned by a correctional officer because she was recently involved with cohorts who used drugs; one of her friends nearly died of an overdose. She answers the questions put to her in a perfunctory way, looking away and sighing as she maintains an icy coolness. Apparently, she never answers the question, "You want to tell me what you are doing here, Caroline?" Her parents sit her down for a talk when they arrive home, and she is equally evasive. She says that the person who took an overdose was "one of those hippie kids . . . I'm not part of that group." She says, "It wasn't my pot." The parents say they understand, and ask her to leave so they can talk alone.

    The parents agree that they do not believe her, and Robert wants to ground her and "clip her wings." Barbara thinks he is too harsh, says that spending a night in jail is enough punishment, and she admits that "we've all had our moments . . . she needs to find out for herself . . . we don't want to push her away." Robert realizes that he has not been privy to the family secret, and Barbara acknowledges that she has known about the drug use for six months.

# *Traffic*: Insight Questions

Caroline gives superficial answers to the drug counselor's questions. How can you tell that she is evasive? What are some signs that someone is withholding information?

Caroline's parents don't believe her. How can they tell that she is lying?

The mother, Barbara, has known about her daughter's drug use for six months. What are your thoughts about parents who do not talk to each other about crucial information?

Do alcohol and drug abuse run in families? How might Barbara influence Caroline's drug use?

Caroline says she is not "one of those hippie kids." She implies that drug addicts are different from other kids. Do you believe that?

# *Traffic* : Discussion Outline

### How directly do the parents speak with Caroline?

The parents are amazingly delicate and indirect. They are so composed that they seem more concerned about losing their composure than about dealing with the truth.

They ask Caroline how well she knows the ill young man, and how well she knows the driver. They did not ask specifically about her drug use, how she spends her time, whether she thinks she has a problem, and what she does with her friends. There is no evidence that they contact other parents. They do not demand answers, nor do they confront her with her lies and their doubts. Their questions are closed ended, and do not readily make room for the truth to emerge. Caroline knows how to talk to her parents; she gives them a small hint of the truth, and then keeps quiet.

The correctional officer at least asks the big [open-ended] question: "You want to tell me what you are doing here, Caroline?" Caroline is too smooth to answer that one.

### How do you contrast Caroline with Gwen in *28 Days*?

In the scene that we viewed from *28 Days*, page 65, Gwen acknowledged that she had a problem and that she had to learn how to avoid drugs. Caroline is not there. She does not acknowledge drug use, does not acknowledge that it is a problem for her, does not acknowledge that she is harming others (even though one kid almost died), and not surprisingly, she does not see the need for help.

### How does Barbara enable Caroline's drug use?

Most importantly, she has known about it for six months and kept it a secret from her husband. She does not support even the mild punishment that Robert suggests, giving as the excuse that she has already suffered enough. Like her husband, she does not insist upon a frank discussion of the problem, but instead lets Caroline leave the room even though she knows that Caroline is lying. She minimizes the problem by saying that she (Barbara) used drugs in college. She suggests a hands off approach which will allow her daughter to do whatever she wants, and allows Barbara the luxury of avoiding unpleasant emotions: "We've all had our moments . . . Lord knows I've tried every drug . . . she needs to figure out for herself on her own . . . we don't want to push her away." These statements indicate that Barbara does not want to take effective action.

*(continued on page 72)*

## Does Robert's approach also have its shortcomings?

Yes, he wants to issue consequences – he wants to clip her wings. Yet he does not insist that Caroline talk honestly about the incident and about her substantial drug problem. He wants consequences but not discussion. He is firm about saying that the family does not 'accept' drug use, but does not go further than that. Furthermore, he minimizes his wife's drug use in college, and when he says, "I don't want to hear about it," he may be saying two things: he does not want to hear excuses for his daughter's drug habit, and he also does not want to hear about his wife's contribution (or his own) to Caroline's drug problem. At the end of the scene he is furious at Barbara for her secrets, and perhaps ashamed of his ignorance.

## Is this parenting typical of the 'Boomer' generation of parents?

The popular press has given ample evidence that young people who grew up in the sixties have difficulties disciplining their own children. When it comes to firmness and clearly articulated values, some of the children of the sixties (who are now parents) waffle. I have worked with many young people who were first introduced to drugs and alcohol by their parents and other close relatives. One young woman I treated got her spending money by surreptitiously selling her father's marijuana.

Another common mistake is for parents to take a legalistic approach, in which they feel that they cannot confront children unless they have proof "beyond a reasonable doubt" of drug or alcohol use. The legal paradigm does not work. Parents must take actions and have discussions based on the evidence at hand, and parents must trust their own judgment. Parents who wait until they have ample proof of misdeeds reward their children for being deceitful. Ultimately, children feel safer if they know that their parents care enough to deal with difficult subjects and take painful actions even when they (the parents) are not sure that they are acting entirely fairly. The parents need to admit mistakes and adopt an attitude of humility, but at the same time not ignore obvious signs of trouble.

# Clean and Sober

**Date of Movie:** 1988

**Actors in this scene:**
Michael Keaton as Daryl Poynter
M. Emmet Walsh as Richard Dirks

**Timing on DVD:**
| | |
|---|---|
| 0:00:35 | Title |
| 1:12:47 | Start |
| 1:16:11 | End |

**Start of scene (VHS):**
1:12:12 after the title
Daryl and his sponsor enter the house.

**End of scene (VHS):**
1:15:36 after the title
Daryl stands at the door of his bedroom, staring in.

**Duration of scene:** 3:24

---

**Summary of Movie:**
A young cocaine addict and hustler checks into a drug rehabilitation clinic. His initial agenda is to avoid the consequences of his addiction, and he gets involved disastrously with another patient. Starting a clean life is more difficult than deciding to quit the drugs.

**Summary of Scene:**
Daryl has just left the drug rehab program, and his sponsor, Richard, accompanies him into his apartment. Richard discards the pills and alcohol that are in the house, and helps Daryl to clean up the mess. After Richard leaves the apartment, Daryl quietly, yet restlessly, contemplates his situation. He does not know what to do with himself, and this nonverbal scene portrays powerfully the emptiness and lack of direction that faces an addict as he gives up one lifestyle and has no idea what a sober life entails.

# Clean and Sober: Insight Questions

Now that Michael Keaton is drug-free and out of the rehabilitation facility, he is back in his apartment. Based on what you see in this clip, and what you might imagine, describe his emotional state. What mood does the music convey?

Once drugs are no longer a part of a lifestyle, how do people spend their time?

The sponsor, Richard, seems matter-of-fact and almost casual, yet is also very direct about cleaning out the apartment. He does not lecture or plead. What message does Richard give to Daryl?

What would you surmise about Daryl's friends? Who should he call for help or companionship?

As you view this scene, with what memories do you assume that Daryl is dealing?

## *Clean and Sober*: Discussion Outline

Daryl tells Richard, his sponsor, that the cops have searched his apartment. What is the significance of Richard's searching the apartment himself?

First, he does not trust Daryl's words. He relies on actions. He shows this addicted person that he has to take strong action to overcome his addiction.

Second, he shows that he cares in a meaningful way. He does not accept bland reassurance, but takes the time and effort to search thoroughly for drugs. He even uses a mini-vacuum to remove cocaine powder, and he insists that Daryl screen his telephone calls. He is serious about recovery. His approach contrasts with that of the parents in *Traffic*, page 69.

Third, he knows and demonstrates that drug addiction involves more than one drug. Consequently, he discards prescriptions of many varieties, and he pours out the booze. While many alcoholics just abuse alcohol, the majority of drug addicts use more than one drug. They engage in polydrug abuse or polydrug dependence. They may use heroin, morphine, prescription opiates, cocaine, marijuana, alcohol, benzodiazepines, stimulants, and others. They may prefer one drug, but will abuse several. Most addicts also smoke cigarettes.

Fourth, he knows that addicts get desperate, and may use anything to get high.

## What do you make of his apartment?

Drug addiction is an all-consuming illness. He neglects dirty dishes and rotting food. His chemicals of abuse are scattered everywhere. His life and his apartment are in disorder.

## How has addiction affected other parts of his life?

The sponsor correctly assumes that his social life and work life have also been devastated by addiction. When he states, "most of your friends are sellin' drugs," he points out that there is very little to distinguish between drug users, friends, and drug dealers. Drug dealing supports drug use, and drug users' lives revolve around drugs. (See the definition of Drug Dependence, page 64.) It is hard for them to have lives outside of drugs.

*(continued on page 76)*

## How does the sponsor's approach accord with the 12-step program?

His actions are consistent with Alcoholics Anonymous (AA) and Narcotics Anonymous (NA), especially the notion that Daryl's life is unmanageable, and that he needs to take one step at a time. Richard helps with the practical steps (and does not "let up" when Daryl gets irritated):

- He cleans the apartment.
- He discards pills.
- He pours out alcoholic beverages.
- He sets up an answering machine.
- He gives him a list of meetings and tells him to use it.
- He recommends talking honestly with his boss.
- He tells Daryl that dancing around a problem will become an excuse to get high.

## What do you think of the sponsor?

He seems terrific, and a good match for Daryl. He is helpful but does not try to run his life. Contrast this scene with the one in the movie in which Daryl tries to help another addict get out of her abusive marriage. While doing so, Daryl tries to take over her life and to make decisions for her. He is not ready to be a sponsor.

## What does the quiet scene convey, in which Daryl is alone in the house?

Without the drug scene, Daryl has very little activity in his life. His disease consumed him. He is alone now, without drugs and alcohol, without friends who are sober, and with few inner resources to engage him. At this point in his life, he does not seem serene and peaceful. Instead, his life seems lonely and empty. He has just begun his journey toward sobriety.

# *Affliction*

| | |
|---|---|
| **Date of Movie:** | 1997 |
| **Actors in this scene:** | Nick Nolte as Wade Whitehouse |
| | James Coburn as Glen Whitehouse |
| | Willem Dafoe as Rolfe Whitehouse |
| | Sissy Spacek as Margie 'Marge' Fogg |
| **Timing on DVD:** | 0:01:35     Title |
| | 0:56:09     Start |
| | 0:59:36     End |
| **Start of scene (VHS):** | 0:54:34 after the title |
| | The scene shifts into the farm house and someone says, "How about you Rolfe, are you saved?" |
| **End of scene (VHS):** | 0:58:01 |
| | Glen says (as the camera focuses on the face of Rolfe), " . . . still standing up for your little brother." The scene ends. |
| **Duration of scene:** | 3:27 |

---

**Summary of Movie:**
A deeply troubled small town cop investigates a suspicious hunting death. He gradually becomes unhinged, as his marriage disintegrates, his mother dies, and his alcoholic father continues to ruin all of his children's lives.

**Summary of Scene:**
The family gathers at the run-down family farmstead for a funeral service for the mother. The highly religious daughter tries to carry on in a religious vein, and Wade tries to lead the family in a semblance of a dignified service, while drinking a beer. The patriarch, Glen, grumbles loudly and separately from the family, as he drinks straight whiskey. Glen finally erupts . . . "Not one of you is worth a hair on that good woman's head . . . candy asses . . . Jesus freaks . . ." He provokes a physical fight, dragging them all down to his level.

# *Affliction*: Insight Questions

Have you ever known someone who is alcoholic (dependent on alcohol) who was mean and belligerent when drinking? What was that experience like?

Why are strong religious beliefs helpful for some people who live with extremely dysfunctional families?

Some children of alcoholics, like Rolfe, become very good students and very polite. Why would that pattern of behavior be a useful one in an alcoholic household?

Fighting erupts. In an alcoholic family, why might fighting occur at a funeral?

Glen sits apart from the family. What are the reasons that alcoholics often are emotionally distant from their families?

# *Affliction*: Discussion Outline

Warning! Warning! Warning! This scene is not for the faint-hearted.

After viewing *Who's Afraid of Virginia Wolff*, my father-in-law made the memorable comment, "I know that people live like this, I just don't see why they make movies about them." This is an extraordinarily painful scene, and it is all too real for those who grew up in alcoholic households.

What signs do we see that Mr. Glen Whitehouse is alcoholic? What other signs do we see that he is dysfunctional?

- He drinks straight liquor.
- He remains disheveled even at his wife's funeral.
- He walks with his feet somewhat apart; what physicians call a 'wide-based gait.' Alcoholics damage their cerebellum and thus have difficulty with their balance. They keep their feet far apart to help them maintain their balance.
- He sits apart from the family and friends.
- When he speaks, he has slurred speech, which is characteristic of those who are intoxicated.
- He repeats himself, which is common among those who have brain damage from alcohol.
- He never engages anyone in a true conversation or even an interchange in which he responds as an equal adult.
- He makes extremely hostile insults.
- He gets physically abusive with Wade's girlfriend.
- He engages in merciless ridicule: he makes fun of someone's tone of voice and of his children defending each other; he calls one son a 'smart guy'; he calls his daughter a 'Jesus freak.'

## In what ways do they act as typical 'children of alcoholics'?

The daughter has distanced herself so completely that she mouths clichés about being saved. She is dissociated and is in a parallel universe. She is completely shut off from the pain and rage. She reveals her latent hostility by saying that Rolfe will burn in Hell.

Rolfe has become an academic, and he is the good child -- he refuses a drink. Perhaps by staying good, he strives to avoid his father's wrath. He also seems racked by shame. A visitor indirectly reminds him that he does not visit often enough, and that he does not teach at Harvard. He looks pained. By the end of the scene he looks disgusted and defeated.

*(continued on page 80)*

Wade, the central character in the movie, becomes like his father. He drinks more, he engages in the physical altercation, and he threatens to kill his father if he becomes physically abusive to one of the women. He protects not just the women, but his brother, as perhaps he did several times in their growing-up years.

None of the children mention that their father had a role in their mother's death; either the denial is too great, or they are too fearful of their father. The children are also quite isolated from each other. Sally talks to her brother about being saved, oblivious that 'saved' is a meaningless concept for him. Rolfe makes a joke of his sister's religion. Wade never engages with his siblings, except to intercede on Rolfe's behalf during the fight.

## What do you think of the acting?

I believe it is outstanding. This scene is very believable; their acting is so skilled that it is almost invisible. This movie portrays a classic dysfunctional alcoholic family.

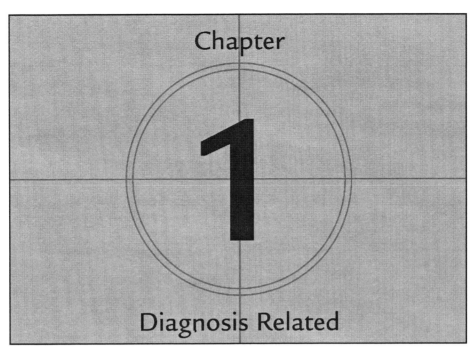

## Section Six - Personality Disorders

*"What if thine own self is not so good? What if it's pretty bad? Wouldn't it be better in case not to be true to thine own self?"*

Des Mcgrath
(Chris Eigeman) in *The Last Days of Disco*

*"You're not dumping me, Buster Blue Eyes."*

Evelyn Draper
(Jessica Walter) in *Play Misty for Me*

---

**Movie Clips:**

| | |
|---|---|
| *The Caine Mutiny* | Paranoid Personality Disorder |
| *Cape Fear* | Antisocial Personality Disorder |
| *Fatal Attraction* | Borderline Personality Disorder, Suicidal Behavior |
| *Play Misty for Me* | Borderline Personality Disorder, Stalking |
| *Anywhere But Here* | Histrionic Personality Traits |
| *The Last Days of Disco* | Narcissistic Personality Disorder |
| *The Fisher King* | Avoidant Personality Disorder, Dependency, Depression |
| *Broadcast News* | Obsessive-Compulsive Personality Disorder |

# Definitions

## Chapter 1- Diagnosis Related - Section Six

### Paranoid Personality Disorder

A pervasive **distrust and suspiciousness** of others such that their motives are interpreted as malevolent, beginning by early childhood, as indicated by at least four of the following:

A. Suspects, without sufficient basis, that others are exploiting, harming or deceiving him
B. Is preoccupied with unjustified doubts about the loyalty or trustworthiness of others
C. Is reluctant to confide in others because of unwarranted fears that the information will be used against him
D. Reads hidden meanings into remarks or events
E. Bears grudges and does not forget insults, injuries or slights
F. Believes others attack his character, and is quick to anger or counterattack
G. Has recurrent unwarranted suspicions of infidelity of spouse or partner

### Borderline Personality Disorder

A pervasive pattern of **unstable relationships, self-image and feelings**, as well as marked instability, plus at least five of the following:

A. Frantic efforts to avoid real or imagined abandonment
B. Unstable and intense relationships alternating between idealization and devaluation
C. Markedly and persistently unstable self-image
D. Self-damaging impulsivity in at least two areas such as spending, sexuality, substance abuse, driving, eating
E. Recurrent suicidal behavior, threats, or self-mutilation
F. Unstable emotions; moods are markedly reactive to situations
G. Long-standing feelings of emptiness
H. Inappropriate intense anger
I. Transient paranoid ideas or dissociation

### Antisocial Personality Disorder

A pervasive pattern of **disregard for and violation of the rights of others** since age 15 years, as indicated by three or more of the following:

A. Failure to conform to social norms with respect to lawful behaviors as indicated by repeatedly performing acts that are grounds for arrest
B. Deceitfulness for personal profit or pleasure
C. Impulsivity or failure to plan ahead
D. Irritability and aggressiveness as indicated by repeated physical fights or assaults
E. Reckless disregard for the safety of self or others
F. Consistent irresponsibility, as indicated by repeated failure to sustain consistent work behavior or honor financial obligations
G. Lack of remorse, as indicated by being indifferent to or rationalizing having hurt, mistreated, or stolen from another

*(continued on page 83)*

# Histrionic Personality Disorder

A pervasive pattern of excessive **emotionality and attention-seeking**, as indicated by at least five of the following:

A. Is uncomfortable in situations in which he or she is not the center of attention
B. Interactions with others are often characterized by inappropriate sexually seductive or provocative behavior
C. Displays rapidly shifting and shallow expression of emotions
D. Consistently uses physical appearance to draw attention to self
E. Has a style of speech that is excessively impressionistic and lacking in detail
F. Shows self-dramatization, theatricality, and exaggerated expression of emotions
G. Is suggestible, i.e., easily influenced by others or circumstances
H. Considers relationships to be more intimate than they actually are

# Narcissistic Personality Disorder

A pervasive pattern of **grandiosity, need for admiration, and lack of empathy** as indicated by five or more of the following:

A. Has a grandiose sense of self importance
B. Is preoccupied with fantasies of unlimited success, power, brilliance, beauty or self-love
C. Believes that he or she is special or unique
D. Requires excessive admiration
E. Has a sense of entitlement
F. Is interpersonally exploitive
G. Lacks empathy
H. Is often envious of others or believes others are envious of him or her
I. Shows arrogant, haughty behavior or attitudes

# Avoidant Personality Disorder

A pervasive pattern of **social inhibition, feelings of inadequacy, and extreme sensitivity** to being judged in a negative light, in a variety of situations, as indicated by at least four of the following:

A. Avoids occupational activities that involve significant interpersonal contact, because of fears of criticism, disapproval or rejection
B. Is unwilling to get involved with people unless certain of being liked
C. Shows restraint within intimate relationships because of the fear of being shamed or ridiculed
D. Is preoccupied with being criticized or rejected in social situations
E. Is inhibited in new interpersonal situations because of feelings of inadequacy
F. Views self as socially inept, personally unappealing, or inferior to others
G. Is unusually reluctant to take personal risks or to engage in any new activities because they may prove embarrassing

*(continued on page 84)*

## Obsessive-Compulsive Personality Disorder

A pervasive pattern of **preoccupation with orderliness, perfectionism, and control**, at the expense of flexibility, openness and efficiency, marked by at least four of the following:

A. Preoccupation with lists, rules, order, details, organization or schedules to the extent that the major point of the activity is lost

B. Perfectionism that interferes with completing tasks

C. Excessive devotion to work and productivity to the exclusion of friendships and leisure activities

D. Over-consciousness, scrupulosity and inflexibility in the arenas of morality, ethics and rules

E. Difficulty discarding worn out or worthless objects

F. Reluctance to delegate tasks or work with others unless they submit to his or her way of doing things

G. Miserly spending style; money is to be hoarded for future catastrophes

H. Rigidity and stubbornness

# The Caine Mutiny

**Date of Movie:**   1954

**Actors in this scene:**   José Ferrar as Lt. Barney Greenwald
Humphrey Bogart as Lt. Cmdr. Philip Francis Queeg
E.G. Marshall as Lt. Cmdr. Challee

**Timing on DVD:**   0:00:19   Title
1:52:17   Start
1:55:57   End

**Start of scene (VHS):**   1:51:57 after the title
In a military courtroom, Lt. Greenwald asks the witness
(Queeg), "Captain, did you ever turn your ship upside down . . . ?"

**End of scene (VHS):**   1:55:37 after the title
The courtroom scene ends, as someone says, "The court is closed."

**Duration of scene:**   4:55

---

**Summary of Movie:**
American officers take command of a U.S. Navy ship during a typhoon in the South
Pacific theater of World War II. They stand trial in a court martial after the fact.
During that trial, the erratic, unpopular Lt. Commander Queeg lets his extreme
suspiciousness become evident.

**Summary of Scene:**
In this famous courtroom scene, Bogart gives one of his best character
interpretations. In the courtroom exchanges prior to this one, Lt. Commander Philip
Francis Queeg sits relatively calmly, but here his words and behavior betray a
different side of him. His eyes dart from side to side, his face contorts and twitches
to reveal torment, and his hands roll the steel balls as his discomfort increases. He
tells a rambling tale, describing his belief that conspiracies abound, that people
hate him because of his adherence to discipline, and that as a result his authority is
undermined repeatedly.

## *The Caine Mutiny* : Insight Questions

Which of the seven symptoms of Paranoid Personality Disorder does Lt. Commander Queeg display?

What are the nonverbal ways that he reveals paranoia?

All of the symptoms of Paranoid Personality Disorder rely on the fact that attacks, suspicions, meanings and others are *unwarranted* or *exaggerated*. Who decides whether they cross the line – whether they are reasonable or unreasonable?

How easy is it to convince a paranoid person that he or she is wrong and in need of help?

What is the difference between paranoia and reasonable suspicion and concern?

# *The Caine Mutiny*: Discussion Outline

The prosecuting attorney attempts to help Lt. Cmdr. Queeg and asks for a brief recess, but Queeg insists on continuing his testimony. Why can't Queeg accept help from his own attorney?

Lt. Cmdr. Queeg cannot trust others; he is as distrustful of his friendly attorney as of his crew. His distrust of everyone, and not just his crew, solidifies our psychiatric opinion (and the opinion of the court) that he has a Paranoid Personality Disorder. When he distrusts several people, then we have proof that Queeg has the problem.

I employ these same considerations when I determine whether a patient has Paranoid Personality Disorder. If a patient's paranoia goes beyond one or two people, and includes much of the world, then I worry that the patient has the paranoia.

I find it very difficult to treat someone who distrusts me. The patient may test me to decide whether I am trustworthy, and this is most commonly done by asking whether I share the paranoid beliefs that the patient has just enunciated. A good clinical approach is to avoid answering the question directly, so as not to be written off. I acknowledge that the fears and pain are real, but I also say that I have no way of knowing the truth.

Perhaps the most memorable part of the scene is Queeg's rolling of the metal balls in his hand. Why is that maneuver so captivating, and consistent with his character?

First, the ball-rolling demonstrates extreme anxiety; he uses the balls as part of his vain attempt to control his agitated emotions. Second, the maneuver demonstrates his ignorance of proper courtroom behavior. He does not realize how his actions affect others; he is preoccupied with the conspiracy. Third, the metal balls act as a barometer of his emotions. When his suspiciousness is at its height, the ball-rolling intensifies.

Queeg becomes especially animated about details such as the quart of strawberries, the missing key, and the shirttails hanging out. Is that consistent with Paranoid Personality Disorder?

Yes, paranoid people often see grand schemes and intricate conspiracies, and they fit the smallest events and snippets of conversations into their conspiratorial beliefs.

*(continued on page 88)*

**Lt. Commander Queeg testifies that he used "geometric logic." Is that comment consistent with his character?**

Herman Wouk, the writer, admirably throws in that phrase for emphasis. As far as I know, geometric logic does not exist, but Captain Queeg is so agitated that he makes up a phrase that seems to make sense.

**Queeg says that all of the officers are disloyal, which contradicts a comment he made in the previous scene, in which he said that only a couple are disloyal. What do you make of his turnaround on this matter?**

As his agitation and paranoia mount, he is no longer able to hide his beliefs. Like other paranoid people, he is grandiose, believing that he is at the epicenter of a vast, intricate conspiracy. His fragile psychological defenses crumble, and he shows his true self; in his mind everyone is out to get him.

**How do family members deal with relatives who have Paranoid Personality Disorder?**

They have difficulty comprehending that the paranoid individual will not change. Family members believe that they can convince him to change, and to see the world differently. Family members believe that if they are loving and insightful, then the paranoid person will relinquish his paranoia. Family members eventually end up frustrated, bewildered, or angry that the paranoid relative does not change. Naïve therapists may have the same reaction.

# Cape Fear

| | |
|---|---|
| **Date of Movie:** | 1991 |
| **Actors in this scene:** | Nick Nolte as Sam Bowden (father) |
| | Robert De Niro as Max Cady |
| | Jessica Lange as Leigh Bowden (mother) |
| | Juliette Lewis as Danielle Bowden (daughter) |
| **Timing on DVD:** | 0:00:58 Title |
| | 1:44:22 Start |
| | 1:51:21 End |
| **Start of scene (VHS):** | 1:43:24 after the title |
| | Max Cady enters the cabin and says, "Evenin' ladies." |
| **End of scene (VHS):** | 1:50:23 |
| | Max Cady, in flames, leaps overboard. |
| **Duration of scene:** | 6:59 |

**Summary of Movie:**
A revengeful psychopath, Max Cady, is released from jail after serving his full 14-year sentence for a brutal rape. While in prison he learned to read, and realized that his attorney had not represented him well and in fact had withheld exonerating evidence from the jury, probably because the attorney realized that Max had a long history of evading arrest for similarly brutal crimes. Max engages in psychological torture of his former attorney, Sam Bowden and his family.

**Summary of Scene:**
Max Cady, unbeknownst to the family, has crept aboard the family's yacht and subdued the father. Max confronts Leigh and Danielle. He asks Danielle if she read the Henry Miller book, Sexus, which he gave to her. He suggestively asks, "Are you offering me something hot?"

Max attempts to rape Leigh, and asks her if she is "ready to be born again." He positions the husband, Sam, to witness the rape, and he kicks Sam in the head. Leigh tearfully tells Max that she empathizes with Max – "all those years locked up in jail . . . I know about loss . . . even losing years . . . I can understand, and share this with you. Whatever you have planned, do it with me, not with her, because we have this connection." Max listens to her, kicks the husband again, and then says, "I will enjoy this all the more." Danielle then throws lighter fluid onto him, and he bursts into flames.

# *Cape Fear*: Insight Questions

Leigh empathizes with him and says that they share a connection. How did Max respond to her?

Did Max seem genuinely concerned with the daughter's welfare, and with her understanding the reading?

If someone does not care how he treats others, what actions is he capable of doing? Have you known anyone who did not care at all about other people?

Max stated that he wanted to become more than human. What does that statement say to you?

Max refers to his grandfather and grandmother with bizarre statements about snakes and strychnine. What is the role of parenting and genetics when it comes to antisocial behavior?

90                    © 2004 Wellness Reproductions & Publishing 1.800.669.9208

# *Cape Fear*: Discussion Outline

**Do you think that Max Cady has Antisocial Personality Disorder?**

He seems to fulfill enough criteria to qualify for the diagnosis. His repeated arrests for rape and other crimes and his planned rapes in this scene make it likely that he fulfills the first criterion, page 82. He fulfills the fourth criterion, since he is extremely aggressive. His brutalizing of the family, including kicking the father in the head, suggests that he fulfills the fifth criterion (disregard for the safety of others). The lack of remorse (seventh criterion) is most striking, and we will discuss it in more detail. He may satisfy the other criteria, but we do not have enough evidence at this point.

**Leigh gives an impassioned plea to Max, as she empathizes with his suffering, and she asks to be raped instead of her daughter. Max is unmoved, and states that he will enjoy raping the daughter all the more. What does his response to her reveal about his character?**

At least twice in this scene Max clearly conveys that he does not care at all about the feelings of others. His suggestive comments to Danielle indicate that he is toying with her and he tortures her psychologically in preparation for raping her. In addition, in the exchange noted above, the mother gives a heartfelt plea, and Max responds with a cold-blooded comment that he will enjoy raping the daughter even more.

Lack of empathy is the hallmark of Antisocial Personality Disorder. That lack of empathy includes a tendency to be callous, cynical, and contemptuous of the feelings, rights and suffering of others. Max is unmoved by the feelings of others because he cannot put himself in their shoes. He does not feel guilt because he is unable to appreciate the pain of others. The only feelings he understands are his own - he mentions his years in prison. The lack of remorse, the aggressiveness toward others, and the disregard for the safety of others all derive from his failure to empathize with others.

Throughout the book I refer to the <u>Diagnostic and Statistical Manual, Fourth Edition</u>. This scene reveals some of the difficulty with that method of diagnosis. As noted above, the DSM IV lists seven criteria for making the diagnosis. Those criteria are based on phenomenology – they enumerate certain behaviors. Critics of the DSM IV approach point out the limitations of a phenomenological approach, and they argue that diagnoses ought to include psychological factors. Critics of DSM IV state that the lack of empathy for others forms the psychological core of those with Antisocial Personality Disorder. These critics believe that the seven criteria for Antisocial Personality Disorder listed in DSM IV miss the point; these seven criteria are byproducts of a more basic problem, which is the inability to empathize with others. Adherents of DSM IV would reply that inability to empathize cannot be measured, and thus ought not to be a criterion for diagnosis. The debate is not resolved.

*(continued on page 92)*

## Are there other names for this disorder?

Yes. At other times, it has been called sociopathy and psychopathy, and individuals with the disorder have been called sociopaths and psychopaths. The reasons for changing the nomenclature are obscure, and relate to public attitudes. After one of these terms comes into use for awhile, it will develop negative connotations. In an attempt to avoid the negative connotations, the nomenclature is changed.

## In addition to lack of empathy, what other qualities characterize those with Antisocial Personality Disorder?

Max says that he is "more than human," indicating that he has an inflated belief in his own powers and greatness. Superficial charm is another common attribute of those with Antisocial Personality Disorder. That charm fools many people, including professionals who interview them.

## Is this condition inherited?

Most mental health professionals believe that terrible upbringing causes people to develop this personality disorder. The accepted wisdom is that these children did not have their basic needs met, and that they had to use all of their psychological and physical resources to care for themselves. As a result, they never developed an appreciation for the needs of others.

Recent evidence indicates that biological or genetic factors may play a role in the development of this disorder. Research has shown that those with Antisocial Personality Disorder have high amounts of serotonin in certain parts of the brain, although the reasons for that are unknown. In addition, adoption studies show that biological children of those with Antisocial Personality Disorder who are raised in adoptive homes have a higher than expected rate of the disorder, implying that the genetics may be more formative than the environment.

The genetic studies are in their infancy and they are not definitive. My judgment is that some tendency toward Antisocial Personality Disorder is inherited, but that upbringing accounts for most of the tendency to develop the disorder. More specifically, I believe that some people are born with an innate tendency toward development of the disorder, and that good parenting will overcome that tendency, whereas bad parenting may compound it. Furthermore, I believe that perfectly normal children (biologically normal) can be raised in a highly disturbed family and can develop Antisocial Personality Disorder even without a genetic predisposition toward it.

# *Fatal Attraction*

| | |
|---|---|
| **Date of Movie:** | 1987 |
| **Actors in this scene:** | Glenn Close as Alex Forrest<br>Michael Douglas as Dan Gallagher |
| **Timing on DVD:** | 0:00:52    Title<br>0:32:11    Start<br>0:35:34    End |
| **Start of scene (VHS):** | 0:31:20 after the title<br>Dan arises from the bed, shedding the embrace from Alex. |
| **End of scene (VHS):** | 0:34:43<br>Alex reveals that she cut her wrists, and Dan then washes them in the sink. |
| **Duration of scene:** | 3:23 |

**Summary of Movie:**
A married man has a weekend fling with a sexy business acquaintance, who then engages in terrifying stalking.

**Summary of Scene:**
Soft music heralds the sounds of warning as Dan Gallagher arises from a bed he has shared with Alex Forrest. He lets her know that their sexual escapades are over, as he returns to his job and his wife. She is enraged, and an ugly goodbye scene ensues, culminated by her slashing her wrists.

# *Fatal Attraction*: Insight Questions

Have you ever known anyone who switched from being loving and tender to hateful and furious? What moods did Alex show in this scene?

What do you think Alex wants from the relationship, and what does Dan want?

Have you ever known anyone who purposefully cut himself or herself? Do you think that Alex wanted to kill herself? If not, what was her purpose in cutting herself?

How responsible does Dan feel for Alex after she cut herself?

How do you think that Alex feels when she is rejected or abandoned by a lover?

# *Fatal Attraction*: Discussion Outline

## What does the term borderline mean?

It is an unfortunate term that is firmly embedded in the field. At one time it suggested that people with this diagnosis inhabited the borderline between psychosis (loss of touch with reality) and neurosis (in touch with reality, but troubled). Today, we do not consider that those who have this diagnosis are on the border of anything.

## Does Alex have Borderline Personality Disorder?

Many mental health professionals suggest that Alex Forest has a severe case of Borderline Personality Disorder. Others disagree. None of the personality disorders have specific and measurable criteria on which to rely for diagnosis. What is *imagined abandonment* and how do we quantify it? What is an *unstable self-image*? When is anger inappropriate, and according to whom? Only criteria four and five, see page 82, utilize criteria that are straightforward. Does it surprise you that clinicians regularly disagree whether someone has the diagnosis of Borderline Personality Disorder?

With that disclaimer, what can we say about Alex's diagnosis? First, we do not know whether she meets the major criterion: *A pervasive pattern of unstable relationships, self-image and feelings, as well as marked instability*. We do not know her well enough to say whether what we see in this scene constitutes a pervasive pattern. We can say that this particular relationship is unstable, and that her feelings in this scene are very unstable.

Looking at the first of nine criteria for diagnosis, it is critical to note that at the start of the scene Alex says, " . . . you run away after every time we make love" and "You're not going to leave." He does not realize how serious she is. This entire scene is predicated on her efforts to avoid abandonment.

Concerning the second point, we certainly see the rapid switch between idealization and devaluation. We witness her blissful embrace (idealization) and the subsequent sarcasm, physical attack, and shouting (devaluation).

It is hard to comment upon the third criterion (unstable self-image), and we see only one glimpse of self damaging impulsivity (sexuality) referred to in criterion four.

The wrist-cutting (consistent with criterion five) and markedly reactive emotions (criterion six) play central roles in this scene.

We see no evidence of emptiness (criterion seven), but she might reveal in an interview that his leaving her triggered an intense feeling of emptiness.

Is her anger intense and inappropriate (criterion eight)? It is certainly intense. The inappropriate question is a fascinating one, and was the central feature of a political debate about the movie. More about that later.

Finally, we do not see signs of paranoia (criterion nine), but an interview might be revealing. She might say that at the time that Dan was leaving she felt outside of her body (dissociated).

*(continued on page 96)*

## Alex frantically tries to avoid abandonment. How does Dan try to end the relationship?

I count five ways, and none of them work. First, he matter-of-factly arises from bed, begins to dress, and prepares to leave. She responds by ripping his shirt, and slapping him. He acts surprised, and she says that she is serious [when she said, "You're not going to leave."] Second, he asks her to be reasonable, but she responds bitterly, letting him know that as far as she is concerned, he only cares about his needs, and not hers. Third, he tries to give her consolation by saying that he likes her and that their relationship could continue if he were not married. She labels that a pathetic comment. Fourth, he acts in a nasty and cruel manner (at her suggestion). She then kicks him, swears and sulks. Finally, he tries to escape by leaving quietly, but she baby-talks, and draws him into helping her deal with her sliced wrists. She has a response to every attempt of his to abandon her.

## What did each of them want from the affair?

He wanted a sexual encounter, and she wanted an intimate, lasting relationship. In an earlier paragraph we pondered whether her anger was inappropriate. From his point of view her anger is highly inappropriate, since he thinks that they both "knew the rules," that it "was understood [that he would return to his family]" and he asks her to "be reasonable." She claims that he tries to "justify himself," and that his explanations are "just pathetic." They had markedly divergent expectations, and it is clear that she believes her anger is appropriate.

## What gender-related debate did this movie stimulate?

Many critics pointed out the dangers of extramarital relationships, and that some women are dangerous stalkers who will not take a hint when it is time to give up on a relationship.

Some feminists and other writers from the female perspective disagreed, and claimed that women such as Alex are unjustly accused of being stalkers, and that men give confusing signals — they lie about their intentions just to convince women to have a sexual relationship. These writers also claimed that men shrink from commitment, and that men with "good marriages" do not have "casual affairs." They claim that Dan deceived both himself and Alex when he claimed that the relationship did not go beyond sex. These critics claim that affairs are not casual, and men such as Dan are so disconnected from their feelings that they do not appreciate or value their relationships with women.

The counterargument to the feminist perspective is that Alex exaggerated the relationship in her own mind and never checked out her assumptions with Dan. These critics of the feminist perspective say that reasonable people in Alex's position would be sad or angry, but they would not act as if they were experiencing catastrophic abandonment. They say that Alex is a sick woman.

I hope that the reader will engage in an extension of this debate, since the debate sheds light on vital issues: the relationship of sex to love, the importance of fidelity within a marriage, gender differences with respect to intimacy, and difficulties communicating about feelings.

# Play Misty for Me

| | |
|---|---|
| **Date of Movie:** | 1971 |
| **Actors in this scene:** | Clint Eastwood as Dave Garver |
| | Jessica Walter as Evelyn Draper |
| **Timing on DVD:** | 0:02:00   Title |
| | 0:38:00   Start |
| | 0:42:16   End |
| **Start of scene (VHS):** | 0:36:00 after the title |
| | Dave Garver says, "The great Errol Garner classic, Misty." |
| **End of scene (VHS):** | 0:40:16 after the title |
| | He hangs up the phone, sits and stares. |
| **Duration of scene:** | 4:16 |

**Summary of Movie:**
A homicidal female admirer stalks a late-night radio disc jockey.

**Summary of Scene:**
Dave comes to Evelyn's house at night, evidently to convince her that he has no intention of continuing their relationship. Evelyn has other ideas: she dresses in a revealing pink dress that she shows off for him, hints about "what a man will go through," calls him darling, refers to herself as a geisha, and she fondles his arms and kisses his hand. Dave is scared and angry, and he says, "I'm just trying to be straight with you . . . I never told you I loved you." She replies, "Not in words, maybe. But there are lots of ways of saying things that have nothing to do with words." When he rebuffs her again, she becomes livid, accuses him of having another woman, calls him sarcastic names ("lord and master . . . Buster Blue Eyes"), and she says, "You're not even good in bed. I just felt sorry for you, that's all." He drives home, only to be greeted by a phone call from her, in which she pleads for forgiveness and a second chance. He tells her that she does not listen. She tells him that she loves him. He hangs up, she redials, and he hangs up again. The chase is on.

## *Play Misty for Me*: Insight Questions

Have you ever had someone come on very strong to you sexually by wearing provocative clothes? What were your thoughts at the time, and later?

Have you ever had a relationship that you wanted to continue, but that the other person wanted to end? If so, how did it feel? What did you want to do?

Dave says that he wants to end the relationship, yet he also said sweet things to Evelyn. Have you been in a relationship when the other person gave conflicting messages? How did you feel?

Did anyone ever call you repeatedly when you did not want him or her to call? Were you scared? What fears (if any) did you have?

Some people do not take a hint; they do not end a relationship when the other person has hinted that he or she wants it to end. Some people cannot handle rejection well. How do you think Evelyn will handle future relationships? How will she handle rejection?

98        © 2004 Wellness Reproductions & Publishing 1.800.669.9208

## *Play Misty for Me*: Discussion Outline

Evelyn wants to seduce Dave, and he wants to end the relationship. How do they convey their messages?

Evelyn . . .
- Dresses seductively in a low-cut pink dress that she later refers to as "my little whore suit"
- Stands appealingly at the fireside
- Welcomes him with a throaty "Hi"
- Prepares a tasty treat of hors d'oeuvres
- Makes suggestive comments about what a man will go through
- Asks him to compliment her appearance as she models the dress
- Gives him expensive shoes as a gift
- Physically sits him down
- Talks about "Madame Butterfly time" when the "neighborhood geisha" removes some clothing

Dave, on the other hand . . .
- Says, "There's something we have to get straight"
- Maintains a serious, worried, bewildered look throughout much of the scene and attempts to be firm
- Tells her she looks "Fine," with no conviction   .
- Asks if they can talk (she cuts him off)
- Tells her to "Stop it"
- Finally says, "I never told you that I loved you . . . I never lied to you"

### One criterion for Borderline Personality Disorder is 'unstable emotions; moods are markedly reactive to situations.' What about Evelyn?

We see that pattern in this scene. She alternates between sweet (overbearing) seductress to a rageful, jilted lover to a pleading pathetic suitor who wants to kiss and make up. This alternation between idealization and devaluation is the hallmark of Borderline Personality Disorder.

### Does Dave give mixed messages that contributed to this mess?

Yes, he ends the previous scene by dedicating a powerfully evocative song to Evelyn. Then he immediately tells her that the relationship has ended.

Furthermore, Evelyn has a point; there are many ways of expressing your love that do not involve words. Dave is evasive when he claims that he never told her that he loved her. In addition, Evelyn was correct when she wondered whether there was another woman in his life. He lied about that fact.

*(continued on page 100)*

99

## What makes Evelyn appear so contemptible?

Her failure to pick up on his clear signals that he is not feeling fondly toward her makes her seem ridiculous. Her horrible comments to him right after her sweet talk ("do you want a Congressional Medal of Honor . . . sitting here in my little whore suit waiting for my lord and master to call . . . you've been keeping me on my back . . . you're not even good in bed . . . I just felt sorry for you . . . you poor pathetic bastard") convey fickleness and excessive cruelty. The phone calls make her seem desperate and shallow.

## What about Evelyn's comment that "You're not dumping me, Buster Blue Eyes"?

I hear four things that set the stage for the subsequent action. First, the threat of abandonment triggers her outrage, just as it does with many people with Borderline Personality Disorder (see criterion one, page 82). Second, the quotation conveys sarcasm, the sort of inappropriate intense anger (criterion eight) that also characterizes Borderline Personality Disorder. Third, it communicates her determination not to let go, that foretells her subsequent stalking. Finally, it hints at threat (the impulsivity common in Borderline Personality Disorder) and goes beyond regret or sadness.

## How do men react to this scene and to the scene from Fatal Attraction?

Interestingly, many men tell me, "I once dated a woman just like that!" They describe a relationship that began with much excitement and great sex. But when the man wanted it to end, all hell broke loose, and he felt bewildered by her frantic attempts to prolong a relationship that he just wanted to end. The men appear shaken by the experience for several years.

## How do women react?

They have mixed reactions. Many believe that the women in these scenes behave badly and in a disordered and dependent manner, while others point out that the men are disconnected from their feelings and they should not be surprised that women experience intensity in the relationship. They think that men should realize that sex and love are connected to one another.

# Anywhere But Here

| | |
|---|---|
| **Date of Movie:** | 1999 |
| **Actors in this scene:** | Susan Sarandon as Adele August |
| | Michael Milhoan as policeman |
| **Timing on DVD:** | 0:00:46    Title |
| | 1:39:51    Start |
| | 1:43:06    End |
| **Start of scene (VHS):** | 1:39:11 after the title |
| | Adele is driving her automobile, weeping, and is pulled over by a policeman for running a stop sign. |
| **End of scene (VHS):** | 1:42:26 after the title |
| | The policeman tells her to have a nice day, and the logo on his squad car is revealed: "to protect and to serve." |
| **Duration of scene:** | 3:15 |

**Summary of Movie:**
Mother and daughter, Ann (played by Natalie Portman) leave Wisconsin to find the good life in California. Adele tries to find herself, and especially has difficulty allowing Ann to mature. They argue frequently, and they find that they can negotiate love and independence.

**Summary of Scene:**
Adele is weeping in her car, as she is pulled over by a police officer for failing to stop at a stop sign. Ann has just informed her that she wants to leave home to attend Brown University. The policeman asks to see her driver's license, but Adele is too distraught to comply. She describes Ann's desire to leave her. She pleads for the officer (a stranger) to acknowledge that she has been a good mother. She hands him her entire purse instead of just her license. He tells her to "watch the signs," gives her confidence that, "you know what to do [about Ann's decision to go to Brown]," and empathetically says that he will let her go, just as she needs to let her daughter go.

# *Anywhere But Here*: Insight Questions

Most people get anxious, scared or tense when a policeman stops them. Adele becomes emotional. Have you ever been around someone who frequently becomes emotional? What is it like to be around that person?

Highly emotional people are often criticized for being shallow - their moods shift rapidly and their opinions change frequently. Does Adele seem shallow? Why or why not?

Emotional or histrionic people often need to be taken care of; they may be dependent. As a result, they become especially emotional when they lose someone important to them. Does Adele have that problem? Beneath all of her feelings, what do you think she is most concerned about?

If you were Adele's friend or therapist, how would you deal with her when her daughter is about to go away to college? What reassurance does she need?

Highly emotional people often dress provocatively. Many people confuse needs for sex with needs for love or attention. Which needs seem most important to Adele, and to the emotional people whom you have known?

# *Anywhere But Here*: Discussion Outline

**Does Adele display the symptoms of Histrionic Personality Disorders?**

Refer to the diagnostic criteria at the start of this section.

1) She is definitely the center of attention. The policeman makes several attempts to get her to show her driver's license, and by the end they shout at each other. Usually the police dominate the scene with their authority, but not here.

2) Sexuality is not immediately evident.

3) Throughout the scene, she shifts emotions, unprovoked by anything the policeman does. When she greets him she says, "Oh my God," as if he is a long-lost friend. She sighs, she shouts, she weeps, and she drops her head onto the car horn. Her emotions seem superficial to me.

4) She drives a Mercedes Benz, she wears bright red fingernail polish, she is well made up, and she carries a flashy purse.

5) The impressionistic style of speech is the hallmark of this disorder, and this scene conveys that trait. Only at the end of the scene does Adele get to the crux of the matter, the detail, when she describes her daughter's desire to go away from home to attend college. Until then we hear vague generalities, including such statements as "I know what you told her . . . you may have been right . . . it hasn't been perfect . . . I make mistakes . . . I'm a little bit selfish . . . I'm a little bit irresponsible and the lights go out . . . it's not easy . . . did she tell you any of the good things I did . . . she's always had a warm house, food, clothing."

6) Theatricality pervades the scene: flinging the purse to the policeman, sighing, rummaging through her purse, emoting with every sentence, and finally her dissolving into tears and not even looking at the policeman when he hands back the driver's license.

7) When the policeman merely repeats her own phrase about her willingness to do anything for her daughter, she decides how to act. He gives advice with a double meaning when he tells her, "Watch the signs, please."

8) She pours out her heart to someone with whom she has had a brief encounter some time ago. She tells him much more than is appropriate.

**Those with Histrionic Personality Disorder often look for emotional reassurance from others. Do we see that here?**

Yes, Adele asks him if her daughter told him about any of her good traits and the good things that she has done as a parent. She clearly is fishing for reassurance and praise. The policeman picks up the hint and he forgives the ticket. Even the slogan on his car conveys his concern: To Protect and to Serve.

*(continued on page 104)*

**Imagine what Adele's romantic relationships are like.**

I suspect that she begins these relationships very intensely, and feels that she has met her soul mate. She throws herself into the liaison with abandon, neglecting other aspects of her life. However, at the merest hint of disapproval or lack of attention she feels devastated and unloved, and requires that he prove his love with extravagant gestures. In the process, she might unleash a stream of hurtful comments, unaware that she is wounding a man whose emotions are not so shallow as hers, and who takes to heart the comments. Their relationship will be intensely romantic yet stormy.

# *The Last Days of Disco*

| | |
|---|---|
| **Date of Movie:** | 1998 |
| **Actors in this scene:** | Chris Eigeman as Des McGrath |
| | Mackenzie Astin as Jimmy Steinway |
| **Timing on DVD:** | 0:00:33    Title |
| | 1:39:52    Start |
| | 1:42:21    End |
| **Start of scene (VHS):** | 1:39:16 after the title |
| | Two men walk out of a building and put luggage into a taxi as one says, "Let me keep your passport for you." |
| **End of scene (VHS):** | 1:41:45 after the title |
| | A Yellow Cab drives away as one of the male passengers says, "To thine own self be true." |
| **Duration of scene:** | 2:29 |

**Summary of Movie:**
Two young women hang out at a trendy disco in the early 1980s. They look for love from young men who are so shallow, self-centered and aimless that they just might succeed. The film is well written and directed, and is sardonic while also being sympathetic to its characters. The music is well suited to the film.

**Summary of Scene:**
Two young men decide to leave the country rather than testify at a trial of a man who has peddled drugs and exploited their friends. One of the young men leaves behind a girlfriend who is hospitalized. They feel guilt-ridden about not staying to testify, but not guilty enough to change their minds. Des says that he plans to turn over a new leaf when he arrives in Spain. In fact, he plans to turn over "several new leaves." "You know that Shakespearean admonition 'to thine own self be true?' It is premised on the idea that thine own self is something pretty good, being true to which is commendable. But what if thine own self is not so good? Wouldn't it be better in that case not to be true to thine own self?" Jimmy replies that his favorite Shakespearean character is Brutus, who killed Caesar. "The way I see it, Brutus was a friend to Caesar." Des asks incredulously, "By stabbing him in the back, Brutus was a good friend to Caesar?"

# The Last Days of Disco : Insight Questions

What evidence suggests that Jimmy lacks empathy for his hospitalized girlfriend?

In what ways do Jimmy and Des act as if they are entitled to special treatment?

Do they lack empathy for others?

Do Jimmy and Des act arrogantly toward the legal system?

Are they exploitive? Do they take advantage of others?

# *The Last Days of Disco*: Discussion Outline

## What is the distinction between Personality Traits and Personality Disorder?

Personality Traits are "enduring patterns of perceiving, relating to, and thinking about the environment and oneself that are exhibited in a wide range of social and personal contexts." (DSM IV) When these traits become inflexible and maladaptive, and cause significant personal distress or functional impairment, we label them as Personality Disorders.

Therefore the distinction between a trait and a disorder is highly subjective, since it relies on an opinion about the influence of personality on one's functioning and sense of well-being. Clinicians have very different approaches to this problem. Some refuse to label anyone as having a Personality Disorder unless the personality problems are flagrant. On the other end of the spectrum, I have known clinicians who suggest that most patients have a Personality Disorder (especially a Borderline Personality Disorder). Other clinicians "defer" to make a judgment about the existence of a Personality Disorder. When the criteria for diagnosis are vague, the usual result is that opinions are firmly held and divergent.

## Do Jimmy and Des have Narcissistic Personality Disorder?

On the basis of this scene, I do not find compelling evidence that they satisfy at least five of the criteria for the disorder. However, more evidence may convince me that they are suffering from Narcissistic Personality Disorder.

I would say that they have many Narcissistic Personality Traits. They act as if they are "special," they act entitled, they seem to be exploiting others, they lack empathy for those injured by the men who are on trial, and they seem arrogant.

In one aspect, Des does not seem to fulfill the criteria for Narcissistic Personality Disorder. He acknowledges that he needs to change (to turn over several new leaves), and he is shocked when Jimmy suggests that Brutus did Caesar a favor by stabbing him in the back. Most of those with Personality Disorders do not believe that they have problems, and they believe that they do not need to change. Des has an inkling of insight, and because of that might benefit from therapy.

Regardless of the exact diagnosis, they show Narcissistic Traits in their indifference (and lack of empathy) to others, their devotion to their own desires, and their sense of entitlement (believing that they should be allowed to start new lives at the expense of others).

*(continued on page 108)*

## Can people with Narcissistic Personality Disorder be treated?

Medicine does not help treat those with Personality Disorders. Psychotherapy is the treatment of choice, even though the results are not spectacular. By definition, those with Personality Disorders do not believe that they have problems, so they do not usually seek help.

However, sometimes they realize that they need help. Those with Narcissistic Personality Disorder may feel empty, bored and depressed, and they may seek help at those times. They do not seek help because of their Personality Disorder per se, but instead they seek help for some of the consequences of the disorder. The therapy does not cure the disorder but it may relieve some of the most extreme aspects of the behavior. In the case of Des and Jimmy, the therapist would not initially deal with the Personality Traits, but would focus on their sense of unease. The therapist would spotlight their discomfort and unease, and point out that if they behave ethically they would feel better about themselves. The therapist would also point out that they care for the friends that they leave behind, and that they are unlikely to find closer friendships in Europe or any other distant location. In general, the therapist would highlight any moments of guilt, depression or loneliness, and help Des or Jimmy to discover ways to deal with those situations.

# *The Fisher King*

**Date of Movie:** 1991

**Actors in this scene:** Robin Williams as Parry
Amanda Plummer as Lydia Sinclair

**Timing on DVD:**
| | |
|---|---|
| 0:01:20 | Title |
| 1:33:18 | Start |
| 1:38:15 | End |

**Start of scene (VHS):** 1:33:02 after the title
Lydia Sinclair says, "You don't have to say that."

**End of scene (VHS):** 1:36:59 after the title
The scene ends as Lydia says, "You're real," and closes the door.

**Duration of scene:** 3:57

---

**Summary of Movie:**
An arrogant radio talk show host, played by Jeff Bridges, is indirectly responsible for a bloody murder when he dismisses a caller too flippantly. He engages in self-loathing and self-destructive behavior, while Parry, whose girlfriend was killed in the bloody episode, also spirals downward. They emerge from their misery with the help of flawed-but-caring women and by complex symbolic heroics.

**Summary of Scene:**
Parry walks Lydia back to her apartment after their double date in a restaurant. Lydia tells him that he does not need to say nice things to her, that she knows he is attracted to her, and that she anticipates that they will return to her apartment, have coffee, make love, and exchange phone numbers. Furthermore, she expects that he will never call her back and that she will feel like a piece of dirt. He tells her that he just wants a kiss, that he understands that she has few friends and does not feel wonderful about herself -- that she feels alone and separate. Lydia is surprised and pleased that he is genuine, and that he cares for her just the way she is.

109

## *The Fisher King*: Insight Questions

What is it like to be with someone who is so self-conscious that he or she does not stop talking?

Lydia imagines the worst outcome imaginable. How does it affect your actions when you only think about what can go wrong?

Lydia says that she feels alone and separate. When you hear someone criticize herself, how do you react?

If you try to reassure someone that he or she is attractive and loveable, how does he or she often react?

How do you feel if someone does not hear what you say because the other person is self-involved?

# *The Fisher King*: Discussion Outline

## Is Lydia painfully shy, or does she have Avoidant Personality Disorder?

The distinction between normal shyness, Avoidant Personality Traits, and Avoidant Personality Disorder is made on the basis of dimensions. Symptomatically, they are similar. The three states exist along a continuum, with the most severe being Avoidant Personality Disorder. Normal shyness involves those feelings of being reluctant to reveal oneself to a stranger. It is normal, and probably useful to be shy when meeting people for the first time. In contrast, someone with Avoidant Personality Traits is more shy than the average person and avoids personal involvement more than the average person. However, the person with Avoidant Personality Traits is not impaired by these traits and can function fairly well in society. This person can develop intimate relationships, although it may take longer than it would for the average person to do so.

Criteria for Personality Disorders are often vague and difficult to quantify and, as a result, even seasoned clinicians disagree whether some people have a *disorder* or not.

The authors of the diagnostic criteria were cognizant of the diagnostic difficulties, so they have phrased the criteria to require that the pattern be **pervasive**, that the sensitivity be **extreme**, and that the person is **unusually** reluctant to take risks in relationships.

From this scene alone we do not know anything about her occupational status (first criterion, for Avoidant Personality Disorder, page 83), but we can imagine that she prefers to work in an isolated cubicle anonymously, avoids the give and take of a bustling office, and that she also avoids customers and the public. Does she avoid getting involved with people unless she is certain of being liked (second criterion)? In her monologue she anticipates rejection, and she then says, "I don't know why I am putting myself through this; it was really nice to see you."
She makes it clear that unless she can be assured of happiness, she would rather avoid getting involved with Parry, even though she is attracted to him. I believe that she avoids intimacy because she is concerned that she will feel shame (third criterion), since she imagines that he will either not call her after spending the night or does not want to spend the night with her at all. She wonders whether he is diseased, divorced, or married; she gives the impression that she will feel ridiculous when it is all over. She is certainly concerned about being rejected (fourth criterion). Her feelings of inadequacy (fifth criterion) are picked up by Parry when he notes that she does not "feel as wonderful as everybody else" and that she feels "alone and separate." It would not take long in a clinical interview to be certain whether she feels inadequate, and whether she fears shame or ridicule. She conveys social ineptness, and she suggests strongly that she feels inferior (sixth criterion). Is she unwilling to take risks because of fear of embarrassment (seventh criterion)? In this scene she runs away from him because she has talked herself into rejection even before it has happened. She believes that he would humiliate her after they expressed strong feelings for each other.

*(continued on page 112)*

**With that summary, do you believe that she suffers from Avoidant Personality Disorder?**

I do not believe that she does. Someone with that disorder would not be quite so articulate about her fears of rejection, and certainly not on the first date. However, since her shyness seems extraordinary, I conclude that she does not have normal shyness, but instead has Avoidant Personality traits. Those with a full-blown personality disorder are not able to change readily, yet we sense that Lydia is poised for change and that with gentle coaxing and a trusting friend she could emerge from her cocoon.

**What about depression?**

Those with Avoidant Personality Disorder frequently become depressed, and they are especially vulnerable to Dysthymic Disorder (*Ulee's Gold*, page 7). Since Avoidant Personality Disorder is pervasive, and continues for most or all of someone's life, it is easy to imagine that someone with the disorder would despair. People with Avoidant Personality Disorder are especially vulnerable to two symptoms of Dysthymic Disorder – hopelessness and low self-esteem.

**How do you treat someone with Avoidant Personality Disorder or Traits?**

Since it is classified as a Personality Disorder, it is difficult to treat. Nonetheless, five considerations are foremost.

First, realize that development of the therapeutic relationship is crucial when treating people with Avoidant Personality Disorder. They expect rejection and they need to feel accepted by the clinician. Those with Social Phobia fear that they will embarrass themselves, so the clinician must be accepting and must put the patient at ease. (See Chapter 4, especially *Ordinary People (2)*, page 171, *Silence of the Lambs*, page 163 and *A Couch in New York*, page 175.)

Second, do not ignore the depression, if it is present. The depression should be treated appropriately -- with psychotherapy, medicine, or both modalities.

Third, the medicine that is used for Social Phobia can be considered. Most people with Social Phobia are untreated, which may lead to developing an Avoidant Personality Disorder. One study revealed that 40% of those with Avoidant Personality Disorder improved to some extent when they were treated with medicine appropriate for Social Phobia.

Fourth, consider alcohol or drug abuse. Many people use alcohol to lessen their anxiety.

Finally, consider using cognitive therapy. This scene depicts <u>cognitive distortion.</u> Lydia envisions the tender beginnings of a relationship, its flowering, and its collapse, all in one grand sweep of her imagination. To avoid the anticipated pain she does not allow herself to have any of the pleasures of the experience. The cognitive therapist will elucidate the ways in which Lydia's distorted thinking prevents her from developing rewarding relationships.

# Broadcast News (2)

**Date of Movie:**            1987

**Actors in this scene:**     William Hurt as Tom Grunnick
                              Holly Hunter as Jane Craig

**Timing on DVD:**            0:05:07      Title
                              1:23:47      Start
                              1:26:59      End

**Start of scene (VHS):**     1:21:15 after the title
                              Tom and Jane have just left a party and are sitting outside on a
                              concrete wall in their evening attire.

**End of scene (VHS):**       1:24:27 after the title
                              Jane says, "You scared the life out of me," and then walks away.

**Duration of scene:**        3:12

---

**Summary of Movie:**
This drama chronicles the rise of a telegenic though uninformed newscaster Tom
Grunnick, at the expense of his hard working, intelligent, knowledgeable yet
uncompromising mentor, Jane Craig, as well as the funny, sad, under-appreciated
writer, played by Albert Brooks.

**Summary of Scene:**
Just before this scene begins, Jane insists that Tom, a co-worker to whom she is
attracted, leave a high-level diplomatic party in Washington, D.C., because she is
worried that he will discover that she has a condom in her purse, since security
personnel are searching all belongings. Tom embraces her while she discusses
political events. She instructs him to kiss her while he fondles her. He talks about her
[sexual] energy, as she gives a four-point mini-lecture about intimacy. She abruptly
leaves, since she remembers that she promised a male co-worker that she would talk
to him about his television performance. Tom irritatedly wags his finger at Jane as
she runs off and he says that she acts "like everything is settled as soon as you make
up your mind."

# Broadcast News (2): Insight Questions

Jane and Tom have a romantic moment, and she instructs him where to put his hand. How does it feel to have someone tell you how to be sensual?

Jane lectures Tom. What is it like to be with someone who lectures you?

Have you ever spent time with someone who suddenly runs off to another engagement during an important conversation? What thoughts did you have about that experience?

Does Jane seem to be aware of her feelings? Is she able to tell Tom how she feels? What is it like to spend time with someone who never talks about his or her feelings? In contrast, what is it like to spend time with someone who shares his or her feelings?

Jane acted like she was in charge. How do you feel when someone else always decides what to do?

114                    © 2004 Wellness Reproductions & Publishing 1.800.669.9208

# *Broadcast News (2)*: Discussion Outline

**Jane does several things that irritate Tom. Does she have Obsessive-Compulsive Personality Disorder?**

Personality Disorders are frequently defined in terms of the people who surround them. The classic distinction between Neurotic Disorders and Personality Disorders revolved around that premise. Those with Neuroses feel miserable, whereas those with Personality Disorders make people around them feel miserable.

Obsessive-Compulsive Personality Disorder is markedly different from Obsessive-Compulsive Disorder (OCD); we will discuss the differences later.

Jane fulfills the first criterion, page 83, of Obsessive-Compulsive Personality Disorder, preoccupation with lists. During a romantic encounter she delineates four reasons for her actions. She also shows evidence of the third criterion, excessive devotion to work. She talks about political events instead of her feelings for Tom, and she breaks off their sensual scene so that she can ask Aaron how his newscast went. She clearly wanted a romantic evening with Tom, since she packed a condom to prepare for the eventual outcome, yet her work ethic interfered. Her over consciousness (fourth criterion) also appears, since she promised Aaron that she would talk with him (but never promised to talk with him in the midst of a romantic interlude). She is inflexible, a promise is a promise, even though it is a fairly minor promise. Her rigidity and stubbornness (eighth criterion) contribute to her leaving despite Tom's evident wish that she stay. Tom astutely observes, "Don't run off – like everything is settled as soon as you make up your mind."

Jane fulfills four of the criteria for Obsessive-Compulsive Personality Disorder, and so qualifies for the diagnosis. Does she fulfill the other criteria? This scene does not tell us, but other evidence and some speculation help us out. She is perfectionistic, and an earlier scene, one of the more memorable in recent movie history, involves her desire to improve a newscast by adding a last-minute nuance. A devoted flunkey, played by Joan Cusack, races with the videotape through a crowded network in order that the scene go on air, with one second to spare. We do not see any evidence that she has difficulty discarding worthless or worn-out objects (criterion five). Jane displays the sixth criterion – reluctance to delegate tasks unless others bow to her will – throughout the film. She is a tyrant on the job, and we get the clear impression that she does not nurture other employees, and does not allow them freedom to experiment or grow. We do not see any miserly spending (criterion seven), but she does not show much interest in material objects. Her unmarried status surprises no one, as she cares about her work above all else.

*(continued on page 116)*

## Is this a lifestyle or is it a disorder?

As with other Personality Disorders, this distinction is important yet difficult to pin down. Diagnostic criteria suggest that a disorder exists if the symptoms cause significant distress or impairment in social, occupational or other areas of functioning. In other words, it is a disorder if it involves distress and impairment, yet on the other hand it is a viable lifestyle if it reflects her life goals. Despite that distinction, I still do not know if Jane Craig has a Personality Disorder, but I guess that she does since later in the movie she is sad that her personality prevented her from developing the personal relationships that could lead to a happy marriage and a family.

Two traits stand out as being the hallmark of Obsessive-Compulsive Personality Disorder, rigid thinking and isolation of affect. Jane seems rigid; I can imagine her saying "my way or the highway." Isolation of affect means that the person is unaware of feelings – the action is isolated from the feelings. In this scene she is unaware that she alienates Tom, the one person whom she loves. She ignores her feelings for him, and instead rushes off for a work-related matter.

## How is Obsessive-Compulsive Personality Disorder different from Obsessive-Compulsive Disorder (OCD)?

Despite its label, there are no obsessions and compulsions in the Personality Disorder; it is simply a different disorder. The compulsions seen in Obsessive-Compulsive Disorder, such as checking, counting, avoiding germs, hoarding, making things symmetrical, and others, are not present in the Personality Disorder. Similarly, obsessions are not part of the Personality Disorder; people with the Personality Disorder are not preoccupied with germs, symmetry, counting, religious concepts and so forth.

The connection between the two concepts lies in the fact that many of those with OCD seem to have many Personality Traits of the Personality Disorder.

# Chapter 2
## Life Cycle Events

# Section One - Bereavement and Pathological Grief

*"You'll never get it if you don't slow down my friend . . . The Earth revolves around the sun and every day the light hits the Earth at a different angle . . . You know how it is, tomorrow and tomorrow and tomorrow Time creeps on its petty pace . . . "*

Auggie Wren<br>(Harvey Keitel) in Smoke

*Forgive me*
*If you are not living*
*If you, beloved, my love, if you have died*
*All the leaves will fall on my breast.*
*It will rain on my soul all night, all day.*
*My feet will want to march to where you are sleeping,*
*But I shall go on living.*

Nina<br>(Juliet Stevenson) in Truly Madly Deeply,<br>from the Donald Walsh translation of the poem by Pablo Neruda, The Dead Woman

---

**Movie Clips:**

| | |
|---|---|
| *Saving Private Ryan* | Grief and Forgetting |
| *Smoke* | Pathological Grief, Visual Memories |
| *Truly Madly Deeply* | Therapy for Pathological Grief |

# Definitions

## Chapter 2- Life Cycle Events - Section One

### Bereavement
The reaction to the death of a loved one.

### Grief
The reaction to loss, including the death of a loved one, but including other losses such as divorce, leaving friends, loss of job, and many others.

### Pathological Grief
The reaction to loss or death is excessive, and may need professional attention. If the symptoms of Major Depressive Disorder (MDD – see Chapter One, Section One) occur during the period of grief, the diagnosis of MDD is **not** made unless the symptoms extend for at least **two months**.

Other signs of **Pathological Grief** include hallucinations (usually auditory or visual), excessive guilt, desire for death, morbid preoccupation with worthlessness, prolonged impairment, or profound difficulty moving or being active.

### Treatment
Bereavement and grief do not require professional intervention, but pathological grief indicates the need for professional attention. The type of intervention varies with the symptom - suicidal individuals may need hospitalization, those with hallucinations or Major Depressive Disorder may need medicine, and psychotherapy is indicated for nearly everyone with Pathological Grief.

# *Saving Private Ryan*

**Date of Movie:**          1998

**Actors in this scene:**   Tom Hanks as Captain John H. Miller
                            Matt Damon as Private James Francis Ryan

**Timing on DVD:**          0:01:02    Title
                            2:02:58    Start
                            2:06:37    End

**Start of scene (VHS):**   2:01:56 after the title
                            Captain Miller's hand shakes, and Private Ryan asks if he is all right.

**End of scene (VHS):**     2:05:35 after the title
                            Captain Miller declines to talk about his wife, and states,
                            "I want to save this for me." The scene ends.

**Duration of scene:**      3:39

---

**Summary of Movie:**

Some people believe that this is one of the greatest war films ever made. Captain Miller leads a squad of men into France to find Private Ryan and give him (Private Ryan) a ticket home, since his three brothers have been killed. Spielberg, the director, shows us that glory and honor can be dangerous and deceptive. The fighting is gruesomely realistic, the characters well crafted, the cinematography superb, and the story well told.

**Summary of Scene:**

The small American fighting force has prepared for the onslaught of a larger German force, and has a few peaceful moments as it awaits the enemy. Private Ryan tells his Captain, "I can't see my brothers' faces." Captain Miller replies, "You've got to think of a context. You don't just think of their faces. You think of something specific – something you've done together." Captain Miller then describes his memory of his wife in the context of pruning the rose bushes while wearing his work gloves. Private Ryan begins somberly as he recalls an episode with his brothers in which three of them interrupt the fourth brother as he is in the barn having a tryst with a local girl. Private Ryan warms to the story, and the memory is uproariously funny to him, Captain Miller, and the audience. They end on a silent note, as Captain Miller saves his own memory of his wife and the rose bushes for himself, and they hear the first sounds of the oncoming German tanks.

# *Saving Private Ryan*: Insight Questions

Name one or two people that you continue to grieve or events that you grieve (such as a traumatic move, a divorce, or another significant loss).

Private Ryan cannot picture his brothers' faces. Describe some confusing aspects of your own grieving, such as difficulty remembering, feeling cut off or dissociated, or being able to remember only certain feelings and not others.

Private Ryan describes a scene at his home. Describe the visual scene, or draw a picture, that expresses or encapsulates your loss or the unresolved grief.

Captain Miller helps Private Ryan to grieve by telling him how he recalls his wife. How can others help you to grieve?

Private Ryan laughs when recalling his last evening with his brothers, and the laughter helps him to grieve their loss. Describe some funny, hidden or other memories of your own losses.

120        © 2004 Wellness Reproductions & Publishing 1.800.669.9208

# *Saving Private Ryan*: Discussion Outline

**Private Ryan asks Captain Miller for help. Should grieving be done in private or with someone else?**

When the grieving person is stuck, as Private Ryan is, another person can be very helpful. Captain Miller took his concern seriously, and talked about his method of dealing with memories. Sometimes the grieving person does not reach out, no matter how badly he feels. In that situation, the thoughts go round and round without clear resolution. When Captain Miller told how he dealt with his own memories, he created a bond between the two of them, and at that moment it did not matter that one was the Captain and the other was the Private. Captain Miller lets Private Ryan know that they are both human. That allowed Private Ryan to tell his story.

**Captain Miller talked about pruning roses. How was that helpful?**

First, Captain Miller connected emotionally by saying, in essence, that they both had the same struggle. Second, he did not use clichés; he did not say that time would heal all wounds, that it was God's purpose, that he shouldn't worry about it, that he should just focus on the task at hand, or that he should feel lucky to be alive. Those comments give an unintended message - you are wrong to grieve, your feelings are not to be taken seriously, and you are ungrateful. Third, Captain Miller did not give a heavy-handed assignment. Instead, he merely suggested that Private Ryan think about a specific memory.

Fourth, and most importantly, Captain Miller indicated that grief work is very particular. Grief involves specific sights, words, and other experiences. Grief involves conjuring vivid memories and languishing in those memories.

**Why is it useful to recall a specific situation?**

Grieving people need to come to terms with the totality of the deceased person. They need to face all aspects of the deceased; the good as well as bad traits and memories need to be acknowledged. Recalling detailed memories, such as that involving his tussle in the barn with his brothers, allows Private Ryan to remember his brothers both intellectually and emotionally. The memory involved sounds, sights, voices, danger, hilarity, sex, fighting, growing up, fellowship, and lurking military duty. This one episode helped Private Ryan to deal with several concerns at once, and to do so with emotions and not just intellect. Sigmund Freud believed that in order to let go of grief, one first had to recall vividly the images of the deceased person.

*(continued on page 122)*

## Captain Miller just listened. Was that helpful?

In this situation it seemed to be very helpful. Those who are grieving find it comforting to be with someone; they do not necessarily want that person to lecture or give advice. The process of listening to someone is an unspoken affirmation - "I can handle your pain, you are not driving me away with your pain, and you can get past your pain."

## Is laughing part of the grief process?

Yes, grief work is like a roller coaster. The recollections run the gamut of emotions - longing, sadness, wistfulness, rage, silliness, poignancy and everything else. It is vital to focus not just on the grim aspects of the grief; all emotions need expression. Some people are blocked because they do not want to face the hatred or evil in the deceased person, but others are blocked because they do not want to admit the humanity and warmth of the dead person. In this lovely scene, Private Ryan faces both somber and hilarious feeling in the course of a few seconds.

# Smoke

| | |
|---|---|
| **Date of Movie:** | 1995 |
| **Actors in this scene:** | William Hurt as Paul Benjamin |
| | Harvey Keitel as Auggie Wren |

**Timing on DVD:**

| 0:04:33 | Title |
|---|---|
| 0:13:50 | Start |
| 0:17:36 | End |

**Start of scene (VHS):** 0:09:20 after the title
As they view a scrapbook of photographs, Paul says, "It's kind of overwhelming."

**End of scene (VHS):** 0:13:06 after the title
Scene ends as Paul weeps.

**Duration of scene:** 3:35

---

**Summary of Movie:**
This low key film that centers around a smoke shop in Brooklyn owned by Auggie Wren involves a tapestry of lives: a cigar store owner who connects with his ex-wife, a depressive novelist (Paul Benjamin) with writer's block, a black teenager on the run and on the lookout for his father, his father who is trying to rebuild a life, and others who are trying to live with imperfection in themselves or in their loved ones.

**Summary of Scene:**
Auggie Wren shares his photographic scrapbook. He has taken a picture every morning, at the same time, from the same location (standing outside his smoke shop) for years. He shows Paul Benjamin that even as the world seems the same, in fact, it changes in every photograph. Paul realizes that his deceased wife is in one of the photographs, and he weeps. Time passes, his wife was captured on film, and he remembers her.

# *Smoke* : Insight Questions

Auggie tells Paul to slow down. In what situations do you avoid feelings, and rush through an experience rather than slow down and take it to heart?

Paul and Auggie remain silent as they view the pictures. Some people always talk – silence makes them uncomfortable. How do you feel when you sit with someone silently?

What family photographs make you cry?

Movies rarely depict men grieving. In your experience, how do men usually act when they suffer loss? How do men respond when someone tries to help them deal with grief?

Do men need other people to help them with their emotions? How can you help someone to grieve when that person is reluctant to accept help?

# *Smoke* : Discussion Outline

## Auggie tells Paul to slow down. How does that help the grieving process?

Paul has writer's block and he seems sad. Other people express their difficulty with grief in ways unique to them. When grieving is blocked, it is sometimes called pathological grief. In essence, it means that someone is stuck and has not been able to grieve fully and then get on with his life. Auggie tries to help Paul get unstuck - he helps him to grieve. To grieve, he has to slow down and let the memories flood back. He has to allow himself to detach from the present, and slowly, quietly experience the past.

## How does their silence help the grieving process?

Even though they do not speak much, they communicate deeply. Auggie helps Paul to slow down, and then to notice the details - the changing light and the changing personalities. He stands next to him and communicates on a tactile (physical) level. The silence enhances the emotional experience; words often interrupt feelings.

In this scene, the silence forces Paul to appreciate the photographs, and finally to see his deceased wife, Ellen. The silence forces him to face his feelings, and he weeps. We get the sense that the weeping is liberating, and Paul may be more able to perk up, to get on with his writing and his life, and to allow other people back into his life.

## Paul cried when he saw the photographs of Ellen. How potent are visual stimuli?

Each person learns and experiences the world in his or her own way. On average, more people are "visual learners" than they are "auditory learners." Too often, psychotherapy is an exclusively verbal exercise. It is crucial to use visual methods in addition to verbal ones. As a psychiatrist, I evaluate patients visually: how does she walk, how is the eye contact, how alert is she, what is she wearing, where does she sit, and what are her gestures? I have learned to take these observations seriously, and not to focus exclusively on the words.

Even though Paul Benjamin is a writer (and deals mostly with words), it is the photograph that unlocks his tears. Similarly, photographs, visits to cemeteries, and treks to the old family home facilitate the grieving process for many people.

*(continued on page 126)*

## Do men and women grieve differently?

I am unaware of research bearing on this question, so I will rely on my observations. Women are more able than men to turn to each other to help with feelings, including grief. Men, on the other hand, tend to deal with feelings in isolation. In addition, women are more oriented toward words, whereas men are more comfortable with actions. As a result, men have a harder time dealing with grief than do women.

This scene shows how men can help each other with grief. Auggie is physically present for Paul, and he tenderly yet unobtrusively gets Paul to slow down, to appreciate the passage of time, and to face his feelings about his deceased wife. I believe that his quiet presence allowed the scene to work so effectively.

## How is this scene similar to the one from *Saving Private Ryan*?

In both scenes, men helped men to grieve, and in both scenes a very specific memory, in context, moved the grief process forward.

# *Truly Madly Deeply*

**Date of Movie:**          1991

**Actors in this scene:**   Juliet Stevenson as Nina

**Timing on DVD:**          0:04:30     Title
                            0:16:30     Start
                            0:19:18     End

**Start of scene (VHS):**   0:12:00 after the title
                            Nina talks with the psychiatrist.

**End of scene (VHS):**     0:14:48 after the title
                            The psychiatric session ends.

**Duration of scene:**      2:48

---

**Summary of Movie:**
Nina's fiancée (played by Alan Rickman) died suddenly and unexpectedly just before the movie begins. Nina is inconsolable. This sad movie takes a sweet black-comic turn when Alan Rickman and some of his dead friends return to Nina's apartment, while she struggles with her love for him and her growing interest in others, who happen to be alive.

**Summary of Scene:**
Nina has a session with a therapist who remains silent throughout the sobbing, anguishing, raging, drooling, and wrenching outpouring. The therapist's lack of empathy (her silence is interrupted only by the tape recorder shutting off), coldness, and blank expression are astonishing. Nina expresses rage against the living who do not appreciate what they have.

# *Truly Madly Deeply*: Insight Questions

Nina expresses rage toward people who do not appreciate what they have. Describe some rageful or angry feelings that you have when you think about someone who is dead (or who left you)?

As you review your life, can you recall some good times that you did not appreciate – that you took for granted?

The therapist does not speak; her tape recorder makes more noise than she does. Do you want someone (such as a therapist) to react when you are extremely upset, or do you want the other person to remain silent? Why or why not?

The therapist did not touch her, and did not offer a tissue until Nina asked for one. Do you believe that the therapist should be more active by touching her, hugging her, or taking another action?

How can you tell if someone is dealing with loss (is grieving) appropriately?

## *Truly Madly Deeply*: Discussion Outline

### What emotions does Nina display during the therapy session?

Nina experiences sadness, rage, anger, hopelessness, envy, and frustration. She believes that the world is grossly unfair. Perhaps you can label other emotions.

These emotions are very intense, with sobbing, blubbering and a raised voice.

Keep in mind that grieving is not just about sadness, but involves the full palette of human emotions.

In addition, the emotions did not seem to *progress or* to *develop* during the session. Instead, she stayed with the same intense feelings throughout the session, pausing only to catch her breath and to use a tissue.

### Does the therapist facilitate the outpouring of emotions?

The therapist does not seem to have elicited these emotions, to encourage or discourage them, or to influence them in any way. She did not block the emotions, offer a consolation or simplistic solutions; nor did she comment on them in any way. She was neutral – a blank slate or mirror.

### Did Nina make progress in this session, or did she remain stuck?

I have heard intelligent people disagree hotly about the value of this session. I believe that the therapist was useless at best and possibly harmful. During a productive session in the therapist's office, a back and forth dialogue ensues. The therapist clarifies feelings, helps to understand the situation, seeks further information, interprets the comments, and generally collaborates with the patient to make sense out of the session. This therapist did none of that.

An effective therapist knows if the session or comment is helpful, the therapist's intervention leads to a change in affect (feeling state), or a change in understanding. In this scene, the affect did not evolve. Instead Nina engaged in an unremitting emotional catharsis. Nina did not seem to understand her misery at the end any better than she did at the start of the session. There was no evidence that Nina was helped by the session.

Some will argue that Nina was able to discharge her emotions, and they imply that such catharsis is a good thing. Catharsis is not necessarily helpful, and many times we find that catharsis can traumatize the patient. The novel Portnoy's Complaint by Philip Roth is constructed in such a way that the protagonist begins the book on the couch of the psychoanalyst, and the book ends with the analyst saying that they are now ready to begin the work. The body of the novel, which consisted of a recounting of Portnoy's feelings, thoughts and behavior (in other words, his catharsis) was not therapeutic in itself, but merely set the stage for the real work. Similarly, Nina's catharsis is not necessarily beneficial. Perhaps that is why Nina slipped into a state in which she found it comforting to live with dead people (later in the movie).

*(continued on page 130)*

## Is this normal grief?

Good question. At least two bits of evidence suggest that Nina has transcended normal grief, and is now experiencing **pathological grief**. First, she loses touch with reality. Losing touch with reality is not part of this scene, but one interpretation of the movie is that Nina became so distraught that she retreated into a world in which her deceased lover returns, and she is comforted by him. She is delusional. A subsequent scene in the movie is similar to a scene from *The Fisher King*, page 109; a character becomes guilt-ridden for having a good time, and is tortured by flashbacks of the deceased lover.

Second, in this scene she does not move forward. She experiences unrelenting sorrow, and is not able to have any perspective, nor express any hope that she will be able to cope in the future. Being *stuck* is another sign of pathological grief.

## How should the therapist have acted?

I shift gears when I work with a grieving individual. First, I make a special effort to *connect emotionally* with the patient. That effort could take many forms - I may express my condolences or sympathies about the loss or express explicit empathy for the feeling being expressed. People who are in the throes of grief often feel shut off from the rest of the world, and do not believe that anyone in the world cares or understands. It is crucial to break through that emotional distance.

Second, I tend to be *more active* than usual when dealing with someone who is grieving. In other settings it is acceptable or tolerable to remain as passive as the therapist in this scene. Being active in other settings may reinforce the patient's passivity, and may serve to enable a situation in which a patient is not invested in taking the initiative in making therapy work for him or her. The situation is different in a grieving process. An active therapist will ensure that the patient does not get stuck in paralyzing introspection. The activity forces the patient to face issues she may otherwise choose to ignore.

Third, I am more likely to *touch* a patient who is grieving than I would other patients. Usually, touching a patient is frowned upon, since it may signal a sexual overture, or communicate a friendliness that can become a barrier to facing painful topics (which one would prefer to avoid talking to a "friend" about). Touching can be a boundary violation. However, placing a hand on a shoulder or forearm of a grieving patient often feels right, since it reinforces the human connection, at a time when the bereaved person may pull away from other people in an effort to avoid dealing with the pain of loss. The physical touch also lets the patient know that I care, and understand the depth of the loss.

Fourth, I will tend to mention one of the losses in my life if it seems appropriate. I am careful that I do not give the message that my pain is greater than hers, or that mine was equally painful. Also, I assure that I have worked through my own loss, so that the patient is not burdened with my tears or torment. That said, sometimes mentioning an analogous loss from my own life can serve to reinforce the empathy that I try to convey, and to give an inkling how the patient might deal with the grief. In short, I will tend to be "more human" and "more real" when dealing with a grieving patient than I will with other patients.

# Chapter 2

## Life Cycle Events

# Section Two - Families and Life Crises

*"A baby holds your hand and then suddenly there's this huge man lifting you off the ground, and then he's gone. Where's that son?"*

Andre Gregory in My Dinner with Andre

---

**Movie Clips:**

| | |
|---|---|
| *Ordinary People* | Family Conflict |
| *The Graduate* | Coming of Age |
| *My Dinner with Andre* | Adult Development Issues, Intimacy, Fear of Death |

# Definitions

## Chapter 2- Life Cycle Events - Section Two

### Adjustment Disorder
Significant symptoms (emotional or behavioral) that occur within three months of experiencing a stressful event.

### Developmental Stage
In each phase of life, individuals face predictable challenges.

Individuals face stressors (and thus their vulnerability to Adjustment Disorders) depending on their developmental stage. In this chapter, we see individuals facing late adolescent issues of identity (*The Graduate*), later adult issues of permanence and family bonds (*My Dinner with Andre*), and death in the context of rigid family roles (*Ordinary People*).

# *Ordinary People* (1)

**Date of Movie:** 1980

**Actors in this scene:**
Mary Tyler Moore as Beth Jarrett
Donald Sutherland as Cal Jarrett
Timothy Hutton as Conrad (Connie) Jarrett
Richard Whiting as Grandfather
Meg Mundy as Grandmother

**Timing on DVD:**
0:00:40     Title
0:55:04     Start
0:56:59     End

**Start of scene (VHS):**
0:54:20 after the title
Grandpa is taking a photograph of Beth, Cal, and Connie.

**End of scene (VHS):**
0:56:15 after the title
Beth leaves to fix sandwiches.

**Duration of scene:**     1:55

---

**Summary of Movie:**
This film is a superb adaptation of Judith Guest's withering portrayal of a crumbling family in the wake of the death of one of the sons in a boating accident. The story is told through the eyes of Conrad, the guilt-ridden brother of the deceased. Beth is a believable, cold suburban wife and mother, while Judd Hirsch depicts one of the few helpful and sympathetic psychiatrists in films.

**Summary of Scene:**
The entire scene revolves around taking family photographs. The words of affection disagree with the body language, which conveys tension, coldness, distance, and hostility. Grandpa says that the photograph will be a prize winner and makes a hostile joke. The grandparents give precise directions and offer unnecessary advice. When Cal plants a kiss on Beth's cheek for the camera, Grandpa says that he can do better. They push around Connie, the youngest in the group, several times. He folds his arms to prevent any physical contact with his mother. Cal seems oblivious to the building tension as the two competing agendas, Beth's desire to photograph the men and Cal's desire to take a picture of mom (Beth) and son (Connie), play out. Beth's unspoken message is her lack of desire to be photographed with her son. Connie attempts reconciliation quietly by suggesting that Cal give Beth the camera. The scene explodes when Connie verbalizes underlying tension and hostility, telling his father to "give her the Goddamn camera!" This stuns everyone into silence, providing Beth a chance to grab the camera, say "smile," and prepare sandwiches. No one comments on Connie's outburst.

# *Ordinary People (1)*: Insight Questions

In what way do the following characters attempt to control others in the scene?

Beth (the mother)

Conrad

Grandfather

What role does Calvin play (i.e., what is his personality), and how does he appear in this scene? Do you know similar people?

Body language can convey tension between characters. What body language do you notice that conveys tension?

Conrad and Beth conflict with one another. How do they treat each other in this scene?

No one mentions Conrad's outburst. What do you think about their silence?

# *Ordinary People* *(1)*: Discussion Outline

Grandfather makes three comments / questions to grandmother. He asks whether she is aiming the camera properly, holding it level, and focusing it. As he makes those comments he smiles and acts jovially. What is going on here?

The grandfather belittles his wife with these comments by claiming that she is incompetent. He hides this hostility beneath his pleasant demeanor, thus disconnecting his aggression from his outward appearance. The grandmother responds indirectly to the grandfather's hostility by quieting him in the same pleasant tone that the grandfather uses. One wonders if this pattern creeps into long marriages in which resentments fester rather than resolve.

The disagreement between Cal and Beth exploded when Conrad told his father to give Beth "the Goddamn camera." Why did a disagreement over such a minor matter explode so violently?

The explosion was less related to the camera than the subtext. Without expressing it as such, Beth does not want to be photographed with her son, Connie. In the previous photo, she and Connie stood side by side without any sign of comfort or touching. As soon as she grasps that Cal wants to photograph mother and son together, she insists on taking a picture of the three men instead. Her persistence annoys us while she continues to badger Cal, even after he asks her to pose for a couple seconds. We can rationalize Beth's unreasonable actions only if we realize that she desperately hates the idea of being photographed with Connie. Connie recognizes her hostility, and he responds accordingly.

*(continued on page 136)*

135

This scene displays widespread denial. What powerful expressions of emotion are suppressed or denied in this scene?

- Grandfather belittles the grandmother with a smile on his face
- Grandmother is irritated with the grandfather ("Be quiet")
- Calvin crosses his arms and disconnects from others
- Cal plants an antiseptic kiss on Beth's taut cheek
- Beth holds her arms to herself, and stands on the fringes
- Cal comments that the photograph will be a "prize winner" even though both mother and son look tense and distant from each other
- Connie turns away from the parents as they squabble
- Everyone fails to react to Connie's explosion, except with silence
- Beth smiles after the explosion, and admonishes Calvin to smile
- Beth fails to acknowledge that she did not want to be photographed with Connie

How do you imagine it is like growing up in a family in which people do not talk about their feelings or important emotional issues?

Books have been written about the subject. Sometimes the children feel bewildered and awful, but rarely do they know why they feel so badly. Other children may fail to acknowledge their unhappiness until later in life, when they develop anxiety and depression. Another reaction to such an upbringing is the development of substance abuse, while remaining unaware of the connection between the self-damaging behavior and the feelings. This film reveals another pattern in that Conrad is normal on the surface, but the family crisis (his brother's death) causes him to feel suicidal. Children often unconsciously repeat the patterns in which they were raised.

# The Graduate

**Date of Movie:** 1967

**Actors in this scene:** Dustin Hoffman as Ben Braddock
Walter Brooke as Mr. McGuire

**Timing on DVD:**
0:00:48   Title
0:02:55   Start
0:06:35   End

**Start of scene (VHS):** 0:02:07 after the title
Ben sits in his room staring at the fish tank and the camera.

**End of scene (VHS):** 0:05:47 after the title
Ben shuts the door and stands quietly in his room.

**Duration of scene:** 3:40

---

**Summary of Movie:**
Ben, a naïve college graduate, faces his future with deep uncertainty. He is utterly uncertain about his future occupation, as well as his attachments to friends and potential lovers. Mrs. Robinson, a married friend of his parents, seduces him, but he betrays her by falling in love with her daughter.

**Summary of Scene:**
Ben's parents throw him a graduation party, and invite their friends. These adults congratulate Ben on his college successes, giving him advice for the future including . . . "I want to say one word to you, Ben, just one word . . . plastics. There's a great future in plastics. Enough said." All he wants to do is escape the loud noises and unwarranted confidence of his parents' friends.

# *The Graduate*: Insight Questions

In what ways do or did your parents' occupational decisions affect your own choices?

How much do you think accomplishments in high school and college lead to later success?

How important do you think is it to respect or reject some of your parents' values?

Has anyone ever given you firm advice about your future plans? How did that feel? Was it helpful in the short term? In the long term?

At what time or times of life do people agonize about their values and their place in the world?

# *The Graduate* : Discussion Outline

The adults praise Ben's college accomplishments. What are those accomplishments, and how do the adults respond to those accomplishments?

Through the party clatter we hear that Ben:
- won a scholarship
- became managing editor of the college yearbook
- was a track star

The adults see future success, as reflected by :
- the red Alpha Romeo sports car outside
- "chicks" and "teeny-boppers"

The adults shower praise on Ben in the form of advice ("plastics"), comment that they are "Proud, Proud, Proud, Proud, Proud", and shriek their approval. They dress in their finest evening apparel and are well made-up.


## Ben is asked "Is anything wrong?" What do you think is the real answer here?

Ben embraced his parents' values, yet now feels alienated from them and their values. He is in a spiritual crisis, looking for meaning. The fine clothes, household furnishings, drinking, smiles and make-up reflect the plastic in the future that he questions.

He does not seem to suffer from an illness, but rather self-definition. The camera work often reveals Ben in close up, while the others are a distant blurry haze. Similarly, the adoring sounds and clinking glasses blur into fuzzy background rumbling. The close-ups of Ben reveal that he is sweating and breathing hard. From Ben's perspective the world is without clear definition, and experiences existential turmoil.


## Would this graduation party happen today?

I do not believe so. Today, adults are less secure in their opinions, less certain about the future, and more tolerant of differences. The mantra of many contemporary adults is, "I just want my children to be happy." Most parents today are aware of their minimal control over their children's futures.

I believe that Ben's choices and values are more mainstream now than they were in 1967. Many of today's parents eventually embodied Ben's view of the world.


*(continued on page 140)*

## Would Ben exist today?

I doubt it. Young people face significantly different obstacles today than in the late 1960s. Back then, young men faced being drafted to fight a war many of them did not believe in, and some of them had the wealth and opportunity to doubt their roles in the world.

Today, in contrast, the worries of terrorism, illicit drugs, reduced economic opportunities, and cynicism about bureaucracies or globalization overwhelm young people. Today, young people may see Ben as self-indulgent, while others may see Ben as a "whiner." On the other hand, Ben frequently shows up on television reruns of *The Graduate*, and consoles today's youth by letting them know that becoming an adult has always been painful.

## Is the movie completely out of date?

This film created a furious debate upon its release, often pitting generations against one another. Today I think it has less potency to divide generations or people politically. On a spiritual level, I believe it remains a terrific movie. A young man rejects the values of his parents, which are the values that he freely embraced for some time. Now he has to replace those values with something that is more meaningful for him. At the end of the film he and Elaine face each other, and their demeanors become serious. What values will they embrace? True and unarranged love? Work that is not related to plastics? Friendships that do not revolve around booze and tawdry affairs? Those questions will always provoke debate.

# My Dinner with Andre

**Date of Movie:** 1981

**Actors in this scene:** Andre Gregory as himself
Wallace Shawn as himself

**Timing on DVD:** The DVD is not timed. It is the last scene in the restaurant before Wally takes a taxi home.

**Start of scene (VHS):** 1:46:00 after the title
Wally says, "You know, if I understood it correctly, I think Heidegger said..."

**End of scene (VHS):** 1:48:17 after the title
"Where's that son?" Piano music gently begins, and Wally has a bewildered stare.

**Duration of scene:** 2:17

---

**Summary of Movie:**
This film, based on a play, consists of a conversation in a restaurant, in which Andre elaborates on his confusing last few years. He left his theatrical life and traveled abroad, and he let go of his moorings to experience the wonderment of rebirth and surprise. He struggles to shed pretense and fiction and to be aware of himself and others honestly and without deception. The sincerity and openness of their dinner table conversation reflects the mystical experience that Andre put into words. By the end of the evening, despite his comments intended to root himself in day-to-day routines and material pleasures, Wally is a changed man.

**Summary of Scene:**
Wally quotes Heidegger, saying if you are a feeling human being, you are also aware of your path toward death. Andre picks up the theme and suggests that people fear death to such an extent that they grasp at certain events that let them ignore death, such as their success at work, extramarital affairs, and rigid role models. In particular, he states that our notions of ourselves as mother, father and son are momentary and are used to help us avoid thoughts of death. "A baby holds your hands and then suddenly there's this huge man lifting you off the ground and then he's gone. Where's that son?"

# *My Dinner with Andre*: Insight Questions

The fear of death - how much does that preoccupy people? At what age is that fear most acute? Does it diminish or heighten as you grow old?

Andre talks about "that moment of complete forgetting" during the sexual act. He states that it is hard to stay in that moment of forgetting and instead "you start to think about things," such as "what you've got to do tomorrow." How hard is it for you to stay immersed in a feeling and to block out the everyday concerns of life?

How frightening is it for you to "not know what the next moment will bring?"
Are there certain times of your life when you allow yourself the freedom not to plan your day?

Andre stated that people take comfort in "firm ground." What constitutes firm ground for you?

What is it like for you to change roles, such as going from child to adult, or from daughter to mother?

# *My Dinner with Andre*: Discussion Outline

Andre states that people are afraid of staying in "that place of forgetting" because it reminds them that death approaches. How does this relate to mid-life crises and other life crises?

"Mid-life crisis" is not found in the Diagnostic and Statistical Manual, Fourth Edition (DSM IV) but it is a term often used. I believe that people go through most of their lives firmly rooted in the roles and expectations of their subculture. However, at times they become aware of the march of death, and they allow themselves to view the world in a fluctuating and frightening manner.

Roles change most drastically at certain predictable times, such as when you fall in love and form a nuclear family apart from your original one, when you have your first child, when the last child enters school, when the first child leaves home, when the last child leaves home, when retirement looms, and when serious physical illness impacts you. These are the common times of change, when individuals experience life crises.

I worked with one 65-year-old man who developed cancer, and he wanted to speak to a psychiatrist. He was married and devoted to his wife, but he was also homosexual, and had a long-term clandestine relationship with a man. He wanted to live the rest of his life with this man, but did not want to harm his wife, who had treated him well. His cancer made it obvious to him that death was approaching, and that his previous way of relating to the world was not honest or satisfying. His certainties were no longer certain. In Andre's words, "The world comes in quite fast."

I believe that what we call a mid-life crisis may instead be a willingness to face the fact that there is no "firm earth." However clumsily people deal with that realization, they express a desire to embrace the unpredictable nature of life. Of course, it may be the reverse - their crises may involve frenetic activity intended to deny the onrush of aging and death.

How often do patients address these concerns; how often do existential concerns enter the realm of therapy?

In my experience, patients often mention concerns about impending death and shifting roles, but in a much less sweeping or grand fashion than Andre and Wallace deal with it in this movie. People seek therapy in order to deal with depression, anxiety, collapsing marriages, and loss, but they usually do not frame it as impending death and looking for firm foundations as a way to avoid the uncertainties of life. Existential discussions occur more often between lovers and friends, and with a few trusted others.

When I hear someone describe his or her changing roles, extramarital affairs, or disillusionment with work, I look for a bigger picture in the context of that person's life. That is, if a mother feels

*(continued on page 144)*

143

badly about her daughter going off to college, I will ask myself and her why this transition is especially hard for her, given that most mothers handle that situation without seeing a mental health professional. That questioning will lead us into exploring her past. Perhaps she had difficulties when she left home, losses that her daughter's leaving remind her of, feelings that she is losing what she does best (being a parent), and so forth. In other words, I figure out with the patient why this particular life transition is hard to manage. In the background I listen for the themes that Andre Gregory raises - is she clinging to rigid roles to avoid acknowledging the passage of time, or has she made frantic efforts for years looking for firm ground when she knew all along that everything was shifting anyway? Is she afraid of dealing with her true feelings, and afraid of existing in the moment?  What role does her spiritual life play in this struggle?

In short, I am aware of the existential crises, but I typically deal with the issues by looking at day-to-day concerns and decisions.

# Chapter 3

## Healing in Mental Health Settings

*"You make me want to be a better man."*

Melvin Udall
(Jack Nicholson) in *As Good As It Gets*

| **Movie Clips:** | |
|---|---|
| *Birdy* | Hospitalization |
| *As Good As It Gets* | The Right Medicine and a Good Doctor Patient Relationship |
| *E.T.* | Belief as a Therapeutic Tool |

# Definitions

## Chapter 3- Healing in Mental Health Settings

### Hospitalization
Despite the vast improvements in American psychiatric hospitals in the last few decades, the frightening stereotypes persist. The most common reasons for psychiatric hospitalization include suicidal tendencies, threatening others, and neglecting oneself because of psychosis.

### Belief
One's belief in an eventual cure plays an important part in the healing process. Several interrelated factors in these beliefs are: spirituality, the placebo effect, trust in the doctor, and support from friends and family.

# *Birdy*

| | |
|---|---|
| **Date of Movie:** | 1984 |

**Actors in this scene:**  Nicolas Cage as Al Columbato
Mathew Modine as Birdy

**Timing on DVD:**

| 0:00:35 | Title |
|---|---|
| 1:49:55 | Start |
| 1:56:45 | End |

**Start of scene (VHS):**  1:49:20 after the title (this is the last scene of the film)
At the start of the scene, Birdy sits on the floor clasping the leg of the bed.

**End of scene (VHS):**  1:56:10 after the title
Beginning of the credits.

**Duration of scene:**  6:50

---

**Summary of Movie:**
Two boyhood friends are reunited in an army hospital after experiencing physical and psychic traumas in the Vietnam War. Al flashes back to their adolescence when his innocent friend simply wanted to fly like a bird.

**Summary of Scene:**
Al, who has a heavily bandaged face, embraces his mute friend on the floor of his psychiatric cell. Al says, "Nobody listens to anybody any more even if they aren't crazy," and insists on staying with his friend despite urgings from the nursing staff to leave. Al describes memories of burning flesh, and despairs that "they got the best of us." When Birdy finally speaks in a normal voice, Al is incredulous and remarks, "You needed me, didn't you?" When more hospital staff try to remove Al forcibly, the two young men fight back and escape. Birdy happily flies to safety.

# *Birdy*: Insight Questions

Have you ever been inside a psychiatric hospital, either as a patient or visitor? How did the physical setting contrast with the stark room depicted in this scene - which was concrete and steel, lacked furniture, and had a bare floor?

Burly aides tried to remove Al from the premises. What are the visitor policies in psychiatric hospitals, and do patients have legal rights to have visitors?

Al said that if Birdy would not talk "they will keep you forever." On what basis do you think people should be forced to stay in psychiatric hospitals against their will?

Al asks, "What's so good about the . . . world anyway?" How do you answer that question; what are some of the fundamental reasons to live?

At the start of the scene, Al says that no one listens, and later he believes that Birdy started speaking (and ended his mutism) because "You needed me . . . " Do you believe that we need other people in order to heal, and do you believe that mental health professionals listen carefully?

© 2004 Wellness Reproductions & Publishing 1.800.669.9208

# *Birdy*: Discussion Outline

In this scene, Al expresses heartfelt thoughts to his best friend Birdy, touching on despair and reasons to live. Suddenly, Birdy speaks in a normal voice. The implication is that through a combination of deep caring and brilliant insight, symptoms suddenly disappear. Is that plausible?

When I entered the field of psychiatry I believed that theory, perhaps because I watched too many movies. I have read case histories in which such cures occur. Those case histories usually involve a conversion symptom, such as an inability (for psychological reasons) to move the arm, to see, or to talk. Then an insightful professional says something like, "You can't move your arm because you want to hit you mother, and it is forbidden to hit your mother." With that blindingly perceptive insight, the patient moves his arm and talks about his rage toward his mother.

In real life, conversion disorders in which someone experiences an isolated symptom are rare. Rarer still are instantaneous therapies that lead to symptoms disappearing with a few well-chosen words. Therapy instead is a gradual process in which insights gleaned one day are painstakingly appreciated and acted upon over the next several days, weeks and months.

Al says to Birdy, "What's so great about this . . . world anyway . . . we should just hide out and not talk to anybody?" This can be taken two ways - either he questions why he should live and interact with people, or he expresses depressive feelings. What sense do you make of it?

As a professional, I find it very difficult to differentiate between realistic despair about the meaning of life (and many related existential questions) and depression. I try to avoid labeling or in other ways trivializing people's beliefs about the world we live in.

Often, depressed people are so overwhelmed with negative feelings that they view the world with despair. I recommend that clinicians evaluate whether depression is present by looking at the nine symptoms of Major Depressive Disorder (see *The Last Picture Show*, page 3), including sleep and appetite disturbance, energy, concentration and others. If depression is present, then treating it is important (usually with psychotherapy and medicine). If despair is the only symptom
present, then depression is not the diagnosis. But if despair is accompanied by several of the symptoms of depression, then depression may be the diagnosis.

So, despair may be one manifestation of depression, but the clinical diagnosis of depression involves symptoms in addition to despair. One can question the reasons for living whether one is "depressed" or not. But once someone is less "depressed", he or she may be less vulnerable to feeling that life is hopeless.

*(continued on page 150)*

**The mental health professionals are depicted in uniforms, either wearing the full dress military uniform or the starched white of the nurse and aides. What is the director trying to do, and how do you think psychiatric units ought to look?**

I believe that the director is contrasting the plight of two troubled young men with the rigid organization of the hospital (and by implication, the rigid and cold world). The uniforms imply conformity, strict rules, and unoriginal thinking.

Today, most psychiatric units try to add a warm and homelike look, although they do not always succeed. In the 19th century, Moral Therapy successfully implemented the concepts of treating patients as if they were normal, healthy human beings, and they tried not to reinforce that they were sick.

**The implication is that the world is cruel and that the only sane options include escape (either through running away or through remaining silent) or through fighting back physically. How does that contrast with the belief of most mental health professionals, which is that you have to change yourself?**

Some patients take an attitude like, "I am a victim of horrible upbringing and horrible circumstances. I have a right to feel badly, and I am a victim. Poor me."

Mental health professionals do not dispute the facts, but they will challenge the patient to go the next several steps. How did you cope with those circumstances? Were you too dependent or trusting? Is your coping style working? If not, how might you modify your coping style? Even if you were helpless when you first experienced the trauma, you are not helpless now. How can you act more assertively, live a healthier life, and trust people when trust is warranted? Learn how to evaluate potentially dangerous situations, and take safe steps in those circumstances.

In other words, mental health clinicians look toward the future and change, and do not stop when they hear about past stressors.

# As Good As It Gets (2)

**Date of Movie:**    1998

**Actors in this scene:**    Jack Nicholson as Melvin Udall
Helen Hunt as Carol Connelly

**Timing on DVD:**

| | |
|---|---|
| 0:01:47 | Title |
| 1:36:56 | Start |
| 1:41:06 | End |

**Start of scene (VHS):**    1:35:09 after the title
Carol tells Melvin that he looks great.

**End of scene (VHS):**    1:39:19 after the title
Melvin tells Carol, "Maybe I overshot a little — because I was aiming just enough to keep you from walking out."

**Duration of scene:**    4:10

---

**Summary of Movie:**
Hostile, financially successful, obsessive-compulsive writer (Melvin Udall) learns to show compassion after coming to terms with some of his own failings. He overcomes his hostility and helps a beleaguered and beaten gay man (played by Greg Kinnear) and a struggling mother/waitress.

**Summary of Scene:**
Carol and Melvin enter an out-of-town fancy restaurant only to discover that Melvin needs to purchase a sport coat and tie to meet the dress code. He insults Carol, saying that she is wearing a housedress. She then demands that he should compliment her or she will leave the restaurant. With anguish and disclaimers, he states that because of his affection for her he decided to take his medication for his Obsessive-Compulsive Disorder. When Carol asks why that is a compliment, Melvin explains that being with her makes him "want to be a better man."

## As Good As It Gets (2): Insight Questions

Melvin insults Carol, and seems surprised that she is offended. Describe some instances in which you insulted someone without intending to do so.

Carol became furious and demanded a sincere compliment. In what ways do you stand up for yourself when you are hurt, and in what ways do you think you should be more assertive?

Melvin has difficulty giving a compliment. In what ways do you struggle with giving compliments, or in accepting them?

Melvin resisted taking medicine for a long time. What roadblocks do you experience in taking medicine? What keeps you from taking medicine that is prescribed?

Melvin told Carol that she made him want to be a better man. How do others bring out the best in you and make you want to be a better person?

# As Good As It Gets (2): Discussion Outline

Many of those with Obsessive-Compulsive Disorder (OCD) have poor social skills; they are so wrapped up in their obsessions and compulsions that they do not notice or care how they come across to others. In what ways does Melvin show that difficulty?

He orders food by shouting to the waiter who is on the other side of the restaurant. Many compulsive people are so intent on action, on doing or saying certain things, that tact goes out the window. They are often oblivious to the normal human courtesies, to social context, and to others' perception of them. As a result they often make hostile or indignant comments, and consequently ruin many relationships.

## What is the evidence that it is difficult for Melvin to accept a compliment?

Compulsive people have difficulty expressing and seeing the value of feelings; thoughts and actions are much easier to execute than feelings.

It is difficult for Melvin to compliment Carol. Melvin initially tells Carol that his compliment consists of the fact that he decided to take his medicine following their painful encounter Saturday night. Carol tells him that she does not understand why that is a compliment. In a touching line, he tells her that she makes him want to be a better man. When she melts, he responds by getting embarrassed, making jokes, and by showing how painful it is to be sincere and loving.

It is typical of compulsive people to believe that actions (in this case, taking the medicine) speak louder than words (giving the compliment with feeling). He assumes that she will know the feelings behind the action, and does not initially express the feeling. Finally, he is so overwhelmed by Carol's positive reaction to his compliment that he tries to take it back - to undo it - by saying that he "overshot the mark." He did not mean to express his feelings so openly – he wishes to express them minimally – only enough to placate her.

## Melvin has many misgivings about taking psychotropic medicine (that is, medicine that affects the mind). List reasons why someone may want to take, and the reasons that he may not want to take, psychotropic medicine (or any medicine).

Why Melvin may **want** to take medicine:
1. Fewer symptoms, since the medicine, when combined with behavior therapy, has been proven to be effective for OCD
2. Better social relationships, improvement of overall social functioning
3. Less suffering
4. Freedom to choose and not at the mercy of his symptoms
5. Live a more manageable life

*(continued on page 154)*

Why Melvin may **not** want to take medicine:

1. Side effects, including sexual ones
2. Addiction (not true, in this case) or a long-term need (usually true for OCD)
3. Change of underlying personality (not true, but a common fear)
4. Implication to Melvin that he is sick and defective (subjective judgment that I do not share)
5. Loss of free will (autonomy) - he will be at the mercy of the medicine and will not feel normal emotions (not true, but a common concern)
6. Distrust of science or corporations (that manufacture medicine), a bias against putting foreign substances into his mouth, or a related desire to maintain a purity about his body

**For a long time Melvin refused to take the prescribed medicine. What reason did Melvin give for his decision to take the medicine, despite his misgivings?**

He wants to "become a better man" - a powerful statement. The statement is not made in a vacuum - he wants to become a better man because of Carol, and because of his relationship to Carol.

**What actions can the doctor take to make it more likely that Melvin (or any patient) will actually take the medicine that the doctor prescribes? What can the doctor say or do that will convince Melvin to take medicine?**

**Statements** the doctor can make:

1. Explanation of the benefits of the medicine, which symptoms will improve and which will not improve
2. Warn about side effects
3. Give a time frame in which to expect the effects to occur
4. Answer questions about addictive potential, and other questions
5. State how long the medicine should be taken

**Actions** the doctor can take:

1. Be available to respond to telephone calls or emergency appointments
2. Develop a positive relationship with Melvin; answer questions, and understand his fears and concerns
3. Offer choices and options
4. Use language that Melvin understands and yet which is not overly simplistic and patronizing
5. Avoid being distracted by phone calls or other interruptions, have a private place to speak, and dress in a manner that conveys competence yet also approachability

*(continued on page 155)*

In the mental health fields, often people see the psychiatrist for medicine, and see a therapist for psychotherapy. Name some advantages and some disadvantages to that arrangement.

Advantages:
1. Each professional is doing what he or she does best - the psychiatrist is best at prescribing medicine, and the therapist is best at psychotherapy
2. Two different viewpoints can often be useful
3. More cost-effective
4. The psychiatrist may not have time to do psychotherapy

Disadvantages:
1. The two clinicians may not communicate
2. The patient has to repeat the story to both professionals
3. The patient feels fragmented, and is prevented from developing a complete relationship with either professional
4. The psychiatrist may not spend the time or have the skills to develop a positive doctor patient relationship
5. The two professionals may disagree about the best course of treatment, and may undermine each other. The patient may be left in the dark and feel uneasy, and not know why he or she is not getting better.

Sometimes family members or loved ones accompany patients to see the doctor. If Carol and Melvin develop a lasting relationship, she might consider accompanying him to his appointment with the psychiatrist. How might that make the doctor visit more effective?

1. Carol may convey useful information, including an outside commentary on how Melvin functions at home, crucial details about the past and past treatments, and a description of Melvin's functioning when he is feeling well
2. By accompanying Melvin, Carol conveys that she cares about Melvin
3. Carol helps him remember the doctor's instructions
4. Carol assures that Melvin arrives at his appointment on time
5. Carol gives an objective viewpoint as to the effectiveness of the treatment

Some patients object to having family members accompany them for a doctor visit. List some ways in which Carol's accompanying Melvin on his visit to the psychiatrist might make things worse.

1. Melvin may feel that his privacy is invaded (harder to talk with Carol in the room)
2. The discussion may stay superficial
3. Melvin may feel "ganged up on"
4. Melvin may feel demeaned
5. Melvin may have it reinforced that he is the sick one, and that everyone else agrees that he has to change. This emphasizes the sick role.

156

# E.T. The Extra-Terrestrial

**Date of Movie:** 1982

**Actors in this scene:**
Henry Thomas as Elliot
Dee Wallace as Mary
Drew Barrymore as Gertie

**Timing on DVD:**
| | |
|---|---|
| 0:00:33 | Title |
| 1:00:29 | Start |
| 1:02:18 | End |

**Start of scene (VHS):** 0:57:17 after the title
The mother reads to Gertie, "Peter says the Redskins were defeated.."

**End of scene (VHS):** 0:59:06 after the title
Elliot puts his arm around E.T., and mother can be heard reading, "Peter says . . . "

**Duration of scene:** 1:49

---

**Summary of Movie:**
This exhilarating and touching film depicts an alien botanist who is stranded on earth and befriended by 10-year-old Elliott. E.T. learns about earthlings, and Elliot and his family learn about subtler knowledge of love and friendship. Can E.T. survive the inquisitive, scientific and controlling adult humans, or can children who embrace hope and faith save him?

**Summary of Scene:**
In the background of the scene, the mother reads the Peter Pan story to her daughter, Gertie. You hear her talk about the necessity of belief as a powerful healing force. In the foreground, Elliot and E.T. rummage around, and Elliot accidentally cuts his finger. E.T. uses his powers to heal the cut in a miraculous demonstration of the power of belief.

## E.T. The Extra-Terrestrial: Insight Questions

The mother, Mary, reads about Peter Pan's desire to rescue Wendy and the boys, and Elliot wants to rescue E.T.. How strongly do you want to rescue others? Do you have wishes to be rescued?

Mary reads to Gertie. How do you feel when someone reads to you?

In the Peter Pan story, Tinkerbell drinks the poison to prevent Peter from accidentally drinking it. Has anyone ever sacrificed himself or herself for your benefit?

Tinkerbell can recover from the poison if children believe in fairies. Elliot believes in E.T. even though adults and others do not. In your life, how do your beliefs carry you past obstacles? In what other ways have your beliefs changed your life?

E.T. heals the wound with his touch and Elliot seems both awestruck and fearful. How do you feel when confronted with unknown forces or phenomena?

© 2004 Wellness Reproductions & Publishing 1.800.669.9208

# E.T. The Extra-Terrestrial: Discussion Outline

**Beliefs are powerful. If children believe in fairies, Tinkerbell will be saved; if Elliot believes in E.T. then E.T. can heal the cut and Elliot can help E.T.. How does belief affect medical treatment?**

Every good medical study involves placebos, since the wish to get help and to improve is so powerful. Some patients receive active treatment, and others receive placebo. In general, about 30% improvement is seen in the placebo group.

We see the effects of patients' beliefs in all areas of medicine. Some people who believe that they have been given a hex (in a voodoo belief system) have been known to have sudden death even though they have no signs of illness. Those who expect to die have more surgical complications and death from surgery than those who do not expect to die, and others who have lost all hope and "the will to live" have a very high mortality. Conversely, we have all heard cases of those who survive against high odds, seemingly propelled by their desire to live. Others on their deathbed seem able to stay alive until they have said goodbye to everyone with whom they wanted to say goodbye.

**Elliot says "ouch" when he cuts himself, and E.T. imitates the "ouch." E.T. seems to show empathy by repeating Elliot's word and tone of voice. What is the role of empathy in healing?**

This is another large question. Irvin Yalom studied curative factors in group therapy, and found that people improved when they felt that others in the group cared about them in an empathic way. Similarly, I believe that most patients choose their primary care doctors on the basis of finding someone who is empathic, and understands their hurt. In fact, the empathy that a doctor shows may be more important to many patients than the level of technical skill that the doctor possesses. One big study of malpractice suits showed that people were more likely to sue doctors who were cold and unempathic than they were to sue doctors who made mistakes that caused problems, but who were not cold or unempathic. In other words, the relationship with the doctor was more important than the technical proficiency of the doctor in determining whether to sue.

To take another example, we want surgeons (who are sometimes known to be less empathic than other doctors) to understand us in empathic ways. The surgeon needs to know more than the proper surgical technique. The surgeon also needs to be empathic enough so that he or she knows the patient's priorities. Is it important to the patient to live a long life, to look attractive without scars, to minimize bodily disruption (such as catheters and tube feeding), to minimize pain or to maximize the potential to be productive? Each of these goals could be important, and the surgeon needs to know the patient well enough to balance them appropriately.

*(continued on page 160)*

One study of an anti-anxiety medicine (I believe that it was *meprobamate*) showed that the doctors' beliefs played a crucial role. One set of doctors took a cold, scientific approach, and told patients to try this new medicine, since research showed it would help. Another set of doctors said that this new medicine was the most effective one that they had ever prescribed, and that they (the doctors) were quite convinced that the medicine would provide significant relief. Forty percent of the patients treated by the first group of doctors reported that the medicine helped, and 70% of the patients of the latter group improved. As my pharmacology professor, Dr. Louis Lasagna said, "If you're going to prescribe a medicine, at least work up some enthusiasm for it!"

The same principle holds true for psychotherapy. Patients often feel that their depression, grief, anxiety, or other symptoms will continue without end. Patients feel empowered when the therapist expresses hope and confidence. Patients perceive the clinicians' demeanors – their interest, attention, enthusiasm, concern, focus, and ideas. Patients will respond similarly by working at their problems with energy, perseverance, and creativity. Expectations are powerful.

# Chapter 4

# The Therapeutic Relationship

*"Look at me son, it's not your fault."*

Sean Maguire
(Robin Williams) in *Good Will Hunting*

*"...are you strong enough to point that high powered perception at yourself...maybe you're afraid to."*

Clarice Starling
(Jodie Foster) in *The Silence of the Lambs*

---

**Movie Clips:**

| | |
|---|---|
| *Silence of the Lambs* | Establishing the Doctor-Patient Relationship: Honesty |
| *Good Will Hunting* | Establishing the Doctor-Patient Relationship: Sincerity |
| *Ordinary People* | Establishing the Doctor-Patient Relationship: Genuineness |
| *A Couch in New York* | Warmth and Caring Can Overcome Poor Technique |
| *Dressed to Kill* | Boundaries; Psychiatrist Who Is Too Involved |
| *Frances* | The Patient Who Is Famous; Self-Centered Doctor |
| *Grosse Pointe Blank* | Patient with Disturbing Background |
| *Analyze This* | Psychiatrist Who Is Bored |

# Definitions

## Chapter 4- The Therapeutic Relationship

### Therapeutic Relationship
In the initial session, the patient evaluates several aspects of the clinician – warmth, competence, concern, hope, genuineness, and others. On the basis of these factors, the patient decides whether he is able to work with the clinician.

### Therapeutic Technique
Over 250 schools of therapy have been defined. The wise clinician learns more than one technique, knows the limitations of each approach, and does not allow technique to interfere with human connection.

### Healing Factors
In addition to specific healing techniques, non-specific healing factors include empathy, feeling understood, catharsis, and others.

### Therapeutic Mistake
Clinicians make several mistakes - they fail to empathize, forget information, allow interruptions, make inaccurate interpretations, and others. Mistakes are inevitable. The confident clinician acknowledges mistakes, talks about the mistakes with the patient, and apologizes if appropriate.

### Confidentiality
The clinician cannot divulge therapeutic information without the permission of the patient. The most common exceptions (which vary by state) include abuse of children, intent to kill others, and intent to kill the self.

### Boundaries
Boundaries describe the edge of appropriate conduct by the clinician. In general, clinicians should limit self-disclosure, limit advice-giving, refrain from social relationships with patients, and focus relentlessly on therapeutic topics.

### VIPs
Clinicians often violate boundaries when dealing with prominent patients. They become overly friendly, avoid making unpopular insights, act in an overly accommodating manner, and minimize the severity of the problems.

### Comfort of the Clinician
The clinician cannot work effectively if he or she is intimidated by the patient, scared that the patient will commit suicide, furious with the patient, in awe of the patient, or unable to speak forthrightly for other reasons.

# The Silence of the Lambs

**Date of Movie:** 1991

**Actors in this scene:** Jodie Foster as Clarice Starling
Anthony Hopkins as Hannibal Lecter

**Timing on DVD:**
| | |
|---|---|
| 0:00:56 | Title |
| 0:12:25 | Start |
| 0:18:25 | End |

**Start of scene (VHS):** 0:11:28 after the title
Clarice Starling stands in front of the jail cell of
Dr. Hannibal Lecter. He says, "Good morning."

**End of scene (VHS):** 0:17:38 after the title
Clarice walks away from the cell as Hannibal says, "You fly back
to school now, little Starling, fly, fly, fly."

**Duration of scene:** 6:00

---

**Summary of Movie:**
Clarice Starling, a young FBI agent, is assigned to help find a missing woman, and to save her from a psychopathic killer with the help of another inventive killer, Hannibal Lecter. The movie is almost unbearably intense, and it is superbly acted.

**Summary of Scene:**
Clarice needs Hannibal 'the Cannibal' Lecter to help her, and in this scene they test each other, just as patients test clinicians in the first session of treatment. He asks her questions about her credentials, her past, her competence and training, and her willingness to deal honestly with disgusting material. Despite his notoriety, she treats him with courtesy and formality, she compliments his artistic ability and memory, she looks straight at him despite his attempts to intimidate her through his intense staring, and she finally challenges him to turn his "high powered perception" on himself. He ridicules her background, yet she persists with her forthright attempt to get useful information from him. He dismisses her after reminding her that he once ate the liver of a census taker who "tried to test me."

# *The Silence of the Lambs*: Insight Questions

What are common questions that patients ask therapists in the first session? Should the therapist answer them?

Hannibal Lecter asked Clarice Starling what Miggs said to her. Why was that important to him and to their relationship?

What information should a therapist avoid telling a patient in the first session?

Hannibal Lecter speculates about Clarice's background - that she is "poor white trash," that she tries to overcome her poor background, that her father stank from the coalmines, and so forth. What is he trying to do, and how does Clarice handle the questions and comments?

Both Clarice and Hannibal stare at each other. What are they trying to accomplish?

# *The Silence of the Lambs* : Discussion Outline

At the start of the scene, Clarice is at Hannibal's mercy, since she wants something from him and he wants nothing from her. How does she attempt to get what she wants?

This scene is different from many therapy sessions, since he is not asking her for help. Nonetheless, the scene is analogous to an initial therapy session.

She tells him her name, she addresses him with courtesy (Dr. Lecter), and she asks permission to speak with him. She willingly shows her credentials to him, and acknowledges being in training even though he ridicules the notion. She even gives him power by saying that he can judge whether she is qualified to learn from him. All of this is important to do in a first therapy session. As a result of her skill, he gives her an indirect compliment by saying, "That is rather slippery of you, agent Starling."

She does a few more things to establish a working relationship. She compliments his drawing. It is important to deal with the patient's strengths in addition to the weaknesses. She does not show irritation or anger when he baits her with insults about her past. She does not hesitate to repeat the awful statement that Miggs made to her. She knows how Dr. Lecter treated his victims; it is always important to read background information about your clients. She answers questions about Buffalo Bill, demonstrating that they (Clarice Starling and Hannibal Lecter) are partners in this quest.

Finally, she has enough of a bond with him that she pushes him (she tests the alliance). She challenges him to use his high powered perception – "Why don't you look at yourself and write what you see?"

## Hannibal is also evaluating Clarice. How does he do that?

He sees how she reacts to difficult material. First, he tests whether she is honest enough to admit she is a student, and probably wonders if she will apologize or bend the truth. Second, he stares at her in a menacing manner, yet she does not back down. Third, he asks what Miggs said to her, thereby testing her comfort with sexual content. Fourth, he tests her reaction to his initial refusal to take the questionnaire. Fifth, he asks why the murderer is called Buffalo Bill, thereby seeing whether it is an equal enough relationship that they can ask each other for information. Sixth, when she passes all of those tests he goes for the jugular by making informed guesses about her background, and then using that information to embarrass or infuriate her. She is calm, and returns the challenge by asking him to turn his insights onto himself.

*(continued on page 166)*

165

**What has she learned about working with Dr. Lecter (information that will help her in the future)?**

She already knew that he was brilliant, evil, intimidating and clever. In this interchange she learned that they can develop some manner of a mutually useful relationship as long as she treats him with respect, and tells the truth. She knows that sexual themes permeate his view of the world. Most importantly, she finds that he respects her for not backing down, and for going face-to-face with him.

# Good Will Hunting

| | |
|---|---|
| **Date of Movie:** | 1997 |
| **Actors in this scene:** | Robin Williams as Sean Maguire, a psychotherapist<br>Matt Damon as Will Hunting |
| **Timing on DVD:** | 0:00:43   Title<br>1:46:28   Start<br>1:50:38   End |
| **Start of scene (VHS):** | 1:45:42 after the title<br>Will stands at the doorway and watches an argument between two men, and says, "I can come back." |
| **End of scene (VHS):** | 1:49:52 after the title<br>Will and Sean embrace. |
| **Duration of scene:** | 4:10 |

**Summary of Movie:**
Four young men from the working class neighborhood of South Boston hang out together. One of them, Will, is a mathematical genius. A professor at MIT takes it upon himself to get therapy for this angry young man. The therapy scenes between Sean and Will are riveting, as Will tests him with cruel comments, silence, and superficiality. Sean breaks through the brittle exterior and helps Will become less self-destructive and more available emotionally.

**Summary of Scene:**
Sean and Will discuss the contents of Will's file that Sean (Will's therapist) plans to send to the judge for re-evaluation. Sean views photographs of Will in the file that show cuts and bruises, evidently signs that Will was physically abused. Will asks Sean if he (Sean) had ever been abused, and Sean reveals that he, too, had been abused by his alcoholic father. Then Will describes being beaten by his foster father. Will asks whether his file has phrases in it claiming that he has a fear of abandonment or an attachment disorder. Will states that he broke up with Skylar. Sean is not distracted, as he insists on telling Will that it [the abuse] is not his fault. "Look at me son; it's not your fault." Will mumbles, "I'm so sorry."

# Good Will Hunting: Insight Questions

Have you ever seen your file (school, legal, credit or other)? What was your reaction to seeing it?

Once Sean told Will that he [Sean] had been abused, Will opened up about his own abuse. Do you find it easier or harder to talk to someone who has experienced similar pain as yours? Why or why not?

Will talked about fear of abandonment and attachment disorder. In what situations do you use clinical or intellectual terms in order to avoid talking about nitty-gritty emotional events?

Sean tells Will that it is not his fault. Do you feel that you are at fault for some bad situations, even though rationally you know that it is not your fault?

Sean is insistent with Will, and repeatedly says that it is not his fault. What people in your life can be very firm or direct with you? Why do you let them be firm?

# *Good Will Hunting*: Discussion Outline

**What are your reactions to Sean's revealing to Will that he [Sean] has also been abused? What do you think about therapists revealing information about themselves?**

There are positive and negative aspects of self-revelation, with the negative aspect being the ones that most frequently get emphasized. The negative aspects involve boundary violations; the patient gets too much information about the clinician. In those cases, the patient:

- May not want to hurt the clinician
- May feel responsible for the clinician
- May become sexually involved with the clinician
- May get focused on the clinician's problems and not on his own
- May comfort the clinician instead of receive comfort or emotional attention
- May feel ignored
- May experience other problems or conflicts

The positive aspects of self-revelation, which are often underplayed in professional discussions, include the following:

- Development of rapport - "the clinician can understand me."
- Insight - the story illustrates the point better than a dry comment
- Demonstration that the clinician can get beyond a bad situation, so perhaps the patient can too
- Talking about a painful episode demonstrates that anything can be talked about; secrets are not necessary
- In general, stories have many meanings and can convey rich concepts

In this scene, I believe that it was effective for Sean to tell about his own abuse. I base that conclusion on the best data that we have, the patient's reaction. In this scene, Will began on a superficial note, but when Sean told about being beaten by his father, Will readily told about his own abuse, in a manner that was serious.

## Sean holds Will. Do you think that is a boundary violation?

Boundary violations involve using the patient for the clinician's benefit. Although it is risky to embrace a patient, and I do not recommend it often (especially for inexperienced therapists), I do not see signs that this particular embrace was inappropriate. The embrace was for Will's benefit and did not seem to be for Sean's gratification. The hug did not seem sexual. The hug did not seem to be coercive or manipulative. Instead, it seemed like an affirming action for a patient who was aloof and who did not readily accept warmth and understanding from an adult male. It may help him overcome his hostility toward men and toward himself.

*(continued on page 170)*

## Why do I think this is effective therapy?

One paradigm for therapy is the psychodynamic one. In that paradigm, the past illuminates the present, and the relationship with the therapist (what is labeled the transference) resonates with those issues from the past and from the present.

In this scene, we see the following progression. Sean describes his own abuse (powerful transference). Will then describes his abuse (the past). Will mentions breaking up with Skylar (the present) and wonders whether breaking up with her is related to his fear of attachment (effects of the past). Sean tells Will, "It's not your fault." On the one hand Sean is saying that the past is not Will's fault, but he is also, by his insistence, working on the transference — he forces Will to take his struggles seriously. Through his insistence, Will hugs, cries and says, "I'm sorry." He thus concludes by showing that his behavior in the present (his ability to be warm, sincere and regretful with a strong yet comforting male figure) has changed, for the better, as a result of his resolving the transference and his understanding of the past.

# Ordinary People (2)

**Date of Movie:**      1980

**Actors in this scene:**      Timothy Hutton as Conrad Jarrett
Judd Hirsch as Dr. Berger

**Timing on DVD:**      0:00:40      Title
0:16:03      Start
0:20:24      End

**Start of scene (VHS):**      0:15:22 after the title
Conrad rings the doorbell and stands in the hall.

**End of scene (VHS):**      0:19:43 after the title
The scene in the psychiatrist's office ends.

**Duration of scene:**      4:21

---

**Summary of Movie:**
This film is a superb, meticulously drawn adaptation of the book by Judith Guest. The story concerns a well-to-do family whose son drowned. The mother, played by Mary Tyler Moore, is embittered, superficial and controlling, while the father, played by Donald Sutherland, is mild mannered, and tries to mediate between the mother and surviving son Conrad. Dr. Berger, in one of the few film renderings of a thoughtful and helpful psychiatrist, helps the guilt-ridden Conrad come to terms with his brother's death.

**Summary of Scene:**
Conrad arrives at his initial outpatient session with Dr. Berger, and he inadvertently rings the wrong bell and stands at the wrong door. Dr. Berger, who smokes a cigarette and who has a professional yet informal demeanor, asks Conrad why he is coming for help. Conrad explains that he was hospitalized for four months because he tried to kill himself with razor blades. Dr. Berger asks if others are treating him as if he is on stage, and Conrad states that he would like help so that others will quit worrying about him. He says, "I'd like to be more in control." Dr. Berger says, "I'm not big on control . . . control is a tough nut." Conrad is clearly uncomfortable during the session, as he twitches and stares. When Dr. Berger asks about the boating accident during which his brother drowned, Conrad stares blankly, and Dr. Berger changes the subject, probably because he decided that Conrad was unable to deal with that subject.

## *Ordinary People* (2): **Insight Questions**

Dr. Berger reassured Conrad that other people make the same mistake as Conrad did (standing at the wrong door). Other professionals might have handled it differently by asking Conrad how he felt about making a mistake. Which approach do you think is more helpful, and why?

Dr. Berger smokes a cigarette, turns on some music, dresses casually, and has an informal manner. How do you react to more casually dressed professionals as compared to professionals who are more formal in their attire and approach?

When Dr. Berger asked about the details of the boating accident, Conrad became silent and seemed uncomfortable. After several seconds of silence, Dr. Berger changed the subject. When do you want a professional or authority figure to push you to talk, and when should your reluctance to talk be respected?

Conrad says that the purpose of his seeking treatment is to "be more in control." He could have mentioned other reasons, such as wanting to become less depressed or to quit feeling so guilty, but instead he mentioned wanting to be in control. Dr. Berger did not challenge that choice. What is the importance of deciding why he is seeing the psychiatrist?

Dr. Berger asks why Conrad is here (in the doctor's office) and if everything is okay. Conrad then seems to calm down. Why do you think that comment calmed him down?

## *Ordinary People* (2): Discussion Outline

**Dr. Berger reveals much about himself at the start of the scene. What does he reveal, and why is that important?**

Dr. Berger acts casually and is not concerned with stylized trappings. His office has a confusing doorbell and entrance. He plays music (thereby revealing his musical tastes), and he fumbles with the record player. He rummages through his notes and puffs on a cigarette. He uses everyday expressions when he asks if Conrad feels "on stage," at school, and whether others treat him as if he is a "dangerous character." He avoids psychiatric lingo when he states that "control is a tough nut."

I believe that his casual demeanor helps Conrad to feel comfortable - he is not the only one who lacks control in his life. Conrad does not feel silly for wearing school clothes or for carrying a backpack. In addition, the casualness does not in any way suggest that Dr. Berger is uncaring or indifferent to Conrad. On the contrary, he immediately reassures Conrad that other people make the same mistake that Conrad did.

Dr. Berger establishes a real relationship with Conrad that conveys a certain message. Every therapeutic relationship has reality in it - the clinician always reveals something about himself or herself in myriad ways. In this particular real relationship, Conrad knows that Dr. Berger has certain tastes in music, is comfortable making mistakes (and tolerates others' mistakes), uses plain language, and addresses issues directly.

**Every therapeutic encounter requires a focus. How does Dr. Berger focus the session?**

Conrad states that he has no problems, thereby denying that he needs therapy. Dr. Berger challenges that statement by asking why he is at the session if there are no problems. Conrad then acknowledges that he has a problem, and that he wants to be more in control. Dr. Berger recognizes that focusing on control as a goal in therapy is too vague, so he states, "I'm not big on control." That statement is quite challenging, since he is confronting Conrad's stated purpose for seeking therapy. Recognizing that it is a powerful statement, Dr. Berger adds some sugar to the medicine by saying, "But it's your money, so to speak." By that statement he gives the power back to Conrad, and allows him to set the direction of therapy. Dr. Berger's statement to Conrad, "Control is a tough nut," is subtle, and contains two meanings. On the one hand, he tries to get Conrad to attend therapy twice a week, and confronts him with reality - you are working on a difficult problem, so you need to spend enough time at the job (i.e., you have to attend twice a week and cancel a swimming practice). On the other hand, he makes a mildly sarcastic jab at Conrad. Dr. Berger has already told Conrad that control is not an important value, so he is holding Conrad accountable for his choice. In this manner, he nudges Conrad toward reframing his focus in therapy toward something else, such as sadness, grief, family difficulties, or related issues.

*(continued on page 174)*

Every therapy requires an agreement on the focus of treatment. That focus must be renegotiated frequently. The recurring question is, "Why are you here?"

**Dr. Berger asks about the boating accident. After making a superficial reply, Conrad seems to freeze, and cannot answer the question. He looks very tense. Dr. Berger, after a few seconds of silence, changes the subject. What does that tell you about the *working relationship*?**

Dr. Berger gives Conrad a taste of therapy, and informs him how he will work. He defines the working relationship (or what may be called the clinical relationship or working alliance) - how they work together as patient and doctor. In this scene, Dr. Berger demonstrates that he will approach the most difficult subject which is the boating accident. That tells Conrad that part of the working relationship will involve discussing important subjects. Dr. Berger will not allow him to avoid subjects by talking about the weather or about other superficial distractions.

Dr. Berger defines another aspect of the working relationship - he will monitor Conrad's discomfort, and will help him out if his pain becomes too intense. By changing the subject, Dr. Berger realizes that Conrad cannot yet discuss the boating accident. Dr. Berger will raise the subject of the boating accident later in therapy, when they have built a stronger relationship and Conrad is ready to talk about it.

**In what way does Conrad contrast with Benjamin (played by Dustin Hoffman) in *The Graduate* (page 137)?**

Conrad wants to return to his old self, who presumably was a happier and more engaged person; he wants to fit in better so that others are not concerned about him. Benjamin, on the other hand, has fit in too well in college, and he questions the values that he has embraced previously. All of Benjamin's social, academic and athletic successes seem shallow, like plastic. He defines himself as an insider who wants to shed that insider status, and challenge the very foundations of his social fabric. Conrad just wants to be able to embrace his existing community in ways that feel meaningful.

The movies were made at different times; *The Graduate*, page 137, both defined and reflected a cultural shift in the late 1960s when young people challenged fundamental assumptions of American culture. By 1980, more people acknowledged that their unhappiness could not be blamed solely on society — they had to face their own demons. For that reason, Benjamin is angry, whereas Conrad is baffled.

# A Couch in New York

| | |
|---|---|
| **Date of Movie:** | 1996 |
| **Actors in this scene:** | Juliette Binoche as Beatrice Saulnier<br>Stephanie Buttle as Anne |
| **Timing on DVD:** | 0:05:20   Title<br>0:31:18   Start<br>0:33:46   End |
| **Start of scene (VHS):** | 0:25:08 after the title<br>Two young women are talking, and one says, "I imagine him secretive." |
| **End of scene (VHS):** | 0:28:29 after the title<br>The scene ends and Beatrice says, "Yes!" |
| **Duration of scene:** | 2:31 |

**Summary of Movie:**
A morose New York psychoanalyst temporarily abandons his Manhattan practice and apartment. He switches apartments with a woman in Paris who is unknown to him, and who is fleeing the many men who desire her. She finds commitment; he finds love and spontaneity.

**Summary of Scene:**
Even though Dr. Henry Hairston has abandoned his practice for a month, his patients continue to show up for their appointments at his apartment. Beatrice talks to them (they seem to think that she is the substitute analyst) and they find the sessions worthwhile. She becomes intrigued with psychoanalysis, and asks her friend, Anne, to inform her about proper psychoanalytic technique. Anne, who has been in analysis, tells Beatrice that analysts never give advice and never reveal information about themselves ("That would be a relationship!"). She tells her that analysts say very little, except 'yes' and 'umm hmmm'. Sometimes the analyst repeats a word or phrase that the patient has used. Beatrice innocently brings warmth and joy to this sterile technique.

## A Couch in New York: Insight Questions

Sometimes the therapist (doctor, clinician) says very few words. How is that helpful?

How is it useful for a therapist to repeat a word or phrase?

Giving advice may be harmful in some situations. How may it be harmful?

The tone of voice and body language convey many messages. What is the effect of Beatrice Saulnier's tone of voice and body language in this scene?

What is more powerful – Beatrice's technique (repeating words, saying umm hmmm, remaining silent, and saying yes) or her tone of voice and nonverbal communication?

# *A Couch in New York*: Discussion Outline

**Anne says that her analyst repeats a single word very quietly, neutrally, and softly so as not to interrupt her flow of thought. What are your thoughts about that maneuver?**

In the proper context, it is an excellent approach. When you want to gather history or information, your goal is for the patient to describe the story in great detail. It is crucial not to interrupt the flow. Too often, clinicians interject their opinions too soon, before the narrative unfolds.

Furthermore, when listening to the narrative, astute clinicians will listen for odd words, or phrases that are emphasized or are connected with emotion. The patient is busy relating the story, and may be unaware of these nuances. By repeating a word or phrase, the therapist draws attention to the emotionally laden themes. In that way, the therapist allows the flow of the narrative but focuses on the most important material.

**What make this scene humorous?**

Beatrice uses these techniques on Anne before Anne enunciates them, and without Anne's awareness. Beatrice does not interrupt the flow of words, she remains relatively silent, she does not give advice or talk about herself, and she repeats single words or phrases.

In addition, it is humorous for Anne and Beatrice to reduce therapeutic technique to such a simplified level. They speak of analysis with such awe, yet they describe a sterile and primitive approach. They parody the approach by reducing it to its simple core.

**Why is Beatrice such an effective therapist (or analyst)?**

Despite its silliness, this scene makes a strong statement about therapy. The unspoken subtext of this lesson is that Beatrice is so fresh, so impulsive, so warm, and so emotional that even these neutral techniques are anything but bland.

For many years, researchers have debated whether specific or nonspecific factors are responsible for success of therapy. Specific factors include all stratagems of therapy proposed by each school of research. These stratagems include working through transference distortions (analytic approach), elucidating cognitive distortions (cognitive therapy), reflecting on the effect of behavior on others (dialectical behavior therapy), resolving unusual family roles (transactional analysis), and hundreds of others.

On the other hand, some argue that nonspecific factors (which occur in any therapeutic relationship) are most important. These theorists argue that attributes of therapists such as warmth, unconditional acceptance and positive regard for the patient (among other factors) constitute the curative forces.

*(continued on page 178)*

In this scene, Beatrice quickly learns the specific therapeutic tactics (repeat words, say yes, don't give advice, etc.), but her warmth and genuineness shine through. I could easily imagine that she could be an effective therapist because of her nonspecific attributes; her warmth and kind heart could go a long way to helping a beleaguered soul.

I believe that a therapist needs to possess more than warmth alone, but nonspecific factors are important in therapy, and they serve especially important roles at the start of treatment (when a bond has to form), and at times of dealing with crises and disagreements.

Ralph Greenson, in his book entitled <u>The Technique and Practice of Psychoanalysis</u>, argues that every therapeutic relationship involves a *working alliance* (some call it a *therapeutic alliance*). He defines the working alliance as the bond that forms when the patient knows in his or her heart that the therapist truly cares about the patient, and wants the patient to get better. Greenson states, "The reliable core of the working alliance is formed by the patient's motivation to overcome his illness, his sense of helplessness, his conscious and rational willingness to cooperate, and his ability to follow the instructions and insights of the analyst." [Those clinicians working with especially disturbed patients will note that many of them lack the ability to form a working alliance.] In order to engage the patient, the therapist "offers a realistic hope of alleviating the neurotic misery." Greenson then points out that Freud was misunderstood by analysts who adapted an "austere, aloof and even authoritarian attitude." Greenson believes that "neither smugness, ritualism, timidity, authoritarianism, aloofness, nor indulgence have a place in the analytic situation." He believes that "how we work, the attitude, the manner, the mood, the atmosphere" influences the patient. In particular, the therapist should be "natural . . . and human," and should convey "compassion, concern, and therapeutic intent toward his patient . . . He is a physician and therapist, a treater of the sick and suffering." As such, the therapist respects the patient's rights, and concerns himself "with the patient's need for self-esteem, self-respect, and dignity . . . "

In this scene, Beatrice Saulnier embraces the approach that Greenson advocates. The scenes from *Ordinary People*, page 171, with the psychiatrist (Dr. Berger), as well as the one from *Good Will Hunting*, page 167, similarly demonstrate the formation of an initial positive working alliance. In this scene from *A Couch in New York*, Anne rightly warns against forming a social relationship between the doctor and the patient. However, Greenson's comments plus Beatrice's words indicate that effective therapy becomes possible in the context of a strong therapeutic relationship.

## Dressed to Kill

| | |
|---|---|
| **Date of Movie:** | 1980 |
| **Actors in this scene:** | Michael Caine as Dr. Robert Elliott |
| | Angie Dickinson as Kate Miller |

**Timing on DVD:**

| | |
|---|---|
| 0:00:40 | Title |
| 0:08:25 | Start |
| 0:12:05 | End |

**Start of scene (VHS):**  0:07:52 after the title
Kate descends the steps into Dr. Elliott's psychiatric office.

**End of scene (VHS):**  0:11:32 after the title
The scene ends as Dr. Elliott tells Kate what he thinks of her.

**Duration of scene:**  3:40

---

**Summary of Movie:**

Kate, who is in psychotherapy with Dr. Elliott, is brutally murdered shortly after having a sexual encounter with a stranger. Her son helps police track the killer. This movie has many parallels to *Psycho*.

**Summary of Scene:**

Kate enters the apartment that serves as Dr. Elliott's psychiatric office. Dr. Elliott completes his telephone call with another patient, tells Kate that his secretary is on vacation, and he says that he is doing all of the office chores himself. Dr Elliott asks Kate how he is doing. He tells Kate that it is good to see her and that she should enter the office, as he prepares coffee for the two of them. His voice is kind and slightly seductive. Kate talks about her marriage and about her mother's upcoming visit. Dr. Elliott asks, "What are our options?" He directs the conversation to her marriage, says that it is good to hear that her marriage is fine, but then tells her to confront her husband. Dr. Elliott says that she should tell her husband that she is mad at him and she should not snap at Dr. Elliott. He tells her to stop apologizing. He leans forward, he stares at her, and he tells her that there is nothing wrong with her.

## *Dressed to Kill*: Insight Questions

When is it appropriate to offer a patient a cup of coffee, or other beverage, and when is it inappropriate to do so?

Have you ever overheard a doctor or therapist talking to another patient? How did you feel, and what were your thoughts?

If you are a therapist, and a patient asks you if you find him or her attractive, how should you respond?

How should a doctor respond to a patient that he or she finds attractive?

Has a doctor or therapist ever gotten too personal with you? How did you feel about that? How vulnerable do you feel in a doctor's office?

# *Dressed to Kill*: Discussion Outline

Doctors Gutheil and Gabbard distinguish between boundary crossings (benign) and boundary violations (harmful).[1] They define a boundary as the "edge" of appropriate behavior. In both cases, the therapist (doctor, clinician) allows the boundary between therapist and client (or patient) to be broken. What boundary violations or crossings do you notice in this scene? [I usually ask the class or audience to say 'stop' whenever it notices a boundary crossing or violation.]

- The setting is an office in the doctor's apartment. While this arrangement has been considered appropriate in the past, some clinicians believe that such arrangements put the patient in too intimate contact with the therapist's life.
- The doctor talks to a patient on the telephone within earshot of another patient.
- He reaches his arms out to greet her – more like he would greet a close friend or lover rather than a patient.
- He asks her how he [the doctor].is doing. He wants her to praise him.
- The psychiatrist mentions that his secretary is on vacation. He violates two boundaries – he lets it be known that they are in the office alone (and in an intimate situation), and he tells her information about his professional life (i.e., the fact that his secretary is not present) that the patient does not need to know.
- He ushers her into the office with a seductive and playful tone of voice and words, when he says, "The doctor will be with you shortly."
- He serves coffee, thereby giving the impression that this encounter is a social one rather than a therapeutic one. This could be either a boundary crossing or violation depending on the particular circumstances.
- When discussing her mother, he asks, "What are our options?" By using the word 'our' he incorrectly implies that it is a joint decision, and that he is part of her outside life.
- He stares at her in a leering manner.
- He changes the subject abruptly, and does not allow her to set the agenda when he asks, "How are things going with Mike?" This may be closer to a boundary crossing than violation, or it may be poor technique.
- He makes an evaluative statement by saying 'Good' when she says that things are going well with Mike. He passes judgment.
- She asks if she should be mad, and he says 'yeah.' He tells her what to feel.
- He tells her to direct her anger at Mike rather than at him. A better approach is to help her figure out why she is angry at him [Dr. Elliott]. In this scene, he most likely does not want to deal with her anger that is directed at him.
- He is too pushy and directive when he says, "Think where your anger is going."
- He leans forward, adding to the intimacy of the stare.

*(continued on page 182)*

---

[1]Gutheil TG and Gabbard GO, Misuses and Misunderstandings of Boundary Theory in Clinical and Regulatory Settings, Am J Psychiatry 1998; 155:409-414

- He tells her again to stop apologizing. By insisting that she tell Mike that she is mad at him and that he stinks in bed, Dr. Elliott goes beyond any definition of good technique and strong boundaries.

- When he says, "There's nothing wrong with you," he acts more like a lover than psychiatrist. Clinicians should never say that. Patients need to decide for themselves how they feel and how they come across to others.

- It is never appropriate to say that you want to sleep with a patient.

- It is rarely appropriate to say that a patient is attractive. If the patient insists on an answer, the therapist could ask how his opinion would change how she felt about herself, or could ask how others think of her.

- He says that he would not sleep with her because it jeopardizes his marriage. First, he is telling her about the state of his marriage. Second the reason that therapists do not sleep with patients is because it is harmful to patients, and not because it is harmful to therapists. In fact, he implies that he would sleep with her if he were not married.

## Is this scene realistic?

While it is somewhat exaggerated, many of the boundary violations in this scene occur often in the real world. I have found it to be one of the most instructive scenes that I have ever used. The sexual tension adds to the boisterous arguments that this scene engenders. The acting is exquisite.

# *Frances*

| | |
|---|---|
| **Date of Movie:** | 1982 |
| **Actors in this scene:** | Jessica Lange as Frances Farmer |
| | Lane Smith as Dr. Symington |
| **Timing on DVD:** | 0:01:07  Title |
| | 1:12:10  Start |
| | 1:16:01  End |
| **Start of scene (VHS):** | 1:11:03 after the title |
| | Dr. Symington sits down and moves the ashtray. |
| **End of scene (VHS):** | 1:14:54 after the title |
| | The scene ends as Dr. Symington glares at the departing patient. |
| **Duration of scene:** | 3:51 |

**Summary of Movie:**
This movie is a biography of the self-destructive film star of the 1930s, Frances Farmer, who wound up in an insane asylum.

**Summary of Scene:**
Frances Farmer is evaluated for admission to an insane asylum by the chief psychiatrist, Dr. Symington. Dr. Symington has just ushered the patient's mother out of the room, and makes patronizing comments about stresses faced by celebrities. He assures her that she has nothing to be ashamed of. She turns the tables on him — she belittles and intimidates him, she ridicules him for making an inane joke, and even proves to be more facile than he at making psychological insights.

# *Frances*: Insight Questions

How did Dr. Symington indicate that he is in awe of Frances? How did he indicate that he felt important?

How did Dr. Symington try to assert his control near the start of the scene?

What comments did Dr. Symington make that were patronizing, belittling, or overly controlling?

How did Frances turn the tables? How did she take control?

How did Dr. Symington show his anxiety?

# *Frances*: Discussion Outline

## How did Dr. Symington indicate that he had his own unresolved issues?

He referred to her career. He sounded like a 'groupie' – someone who is star-struck over having a VIP (Very Important Person) patient. He admits to following her career, and he smiles in an adoring way. He wants her to admire him, and he desires mutual admiration. He moves the ashtray at the start of the scene in a manner that is overly solicitous. He reveals that he needs her to admire and respect him. His clothes reveal that he already thinks highly of himself. He shows how vulnerable he is – he needs praise or admiration.

## What did he say that enraged Frances?

- He called her a fascinating case. He thereby tells her that she is not human and not unique – she is a case.
- He tells her that he looks forward to solving her predicament. Therapy is a mutual endeavor, yet he says that he is active and she is passive. That is not a helpful approach to any patient; for a strong-willed person like Frances, his comment is like waving a red flag in front of a bull.
- He says that creative people act erratically. He lumps her into a category of people rather than treating her as an individual. In addition, he makes a sweeping generalization that is probably untrue. It also sounds patronizing, in that he seems to take on the role of the apologist for a helpless person.
- He tells her not to feel ashamed. Psychiatrists do not provide absolution. If she feels shame or any other emotion, she should be encouraged to understand that emotion rather than to dismiss it.
- He makes a stupid joke that he has probably made hundreds of times before. Telling a joke is a continuation of his attempt to convince Frances to admire him; he shows his need to be appreciated for his cleverness.

## Is Frances responsible for this disastrous encounter?

No, I do not believe that she is responsible for this failed attempt at evaluation or treatment. She behaved as patients behave – she showed her symptoms. She did what she was supposed to do - she came to a professional for help, and she showed him why she needed help.

*(continued on page 186)*

## How could a therapist have handled this session better than Dr. Symington did?

First, do not fall into the VIP trap. Do not stand in awe of her or indicate that you need her admiration.

Second, avoid the pitfalls noted above. Do not patronize, belittle, de-humanize, or pigeon-hole Frances. Treat her as a person in distress who needs an intelligent and caring professional to help her.

Third, acknowledge, identify, and confront her behavior in the session. Every clinician has his/her own style, but I may say the following to Frances (often in an inquiring, matter-of-fact, or puzzled tone):

- You are standing up. What does that say? Do you want to be in charge?
- You seem to want to take charge, and to break the rules. Is that what got you here? Do you go head-to-head with authority figures? Do you hate to follow rules?
- You called me a veterinarian, and you dropped your cigarette on my desk. Are you contemptuous of me, indifferent to my needs, or furious? What is that about?
- I am perplexed. You say that you want 'a little rest and a little peace and quiet.' Yet you have tried that before and it didn't work, so you came here. So why are you here? Do you want to work on your problems or not?
- You don't have to stay here if it is not helpful for you. If you choose to stay, we need to agree on the purpose of your being here.
- The behavior that I noticed in the last few minutes – your taking charge, your sarcasm, your rebelliousness, and your contempt – are these the type of things that got you here in the first place? Do you want to work on them together?

These comments are intended to be direct, respectful, and blunt. I intend to foster a spirit of mutual inquiry. I want her to know that she is not forced into treatment; if she is in treatment it is because she chooses to get help. I also try to connect her past behavior to her current behavior, including the behavior in the session.

## Who is the better therapist, Dr. Symington or Frances?

While this is a trick question, and a silly one, I find it interesting that Frances is better suited to the therapist role than is Dr. Symington. First, she listens at the start of the session, and allows Dr. Symington to prattle. Second, she confronts his behavior directly, and does not ignore his blunders. Third, she deals with the behavior in the session. Dr. Symington does not grapple with her emotions, but she aptly points out his attitude (his control and professionalism), and particularly the "tiny little beads of sweat on your upper lip."

# Grosse Pointe Blank

**Date of Movie:** 1997

**Actors in this scene:** John Cusack as Martin Blank
Alan Arkin as Dr. Oatman

**Timing on DVD:**
| | |
|---|---|
| 0:01:12 | Title |
| 0:11:55 | Start |
| 0:16:10 | End |

**Start of scene (VHS):** 0:10:43 after the title
Martin talks to his psychiatrist, Dr. Oatman, and says, "I got invited to my 10th high school reunion."

**End of scene (VHS):** 0:14:58 after the title
The scene ends as Martin leaves the office and Dr. Oatman leans against the wall, bows his head, and grunts.

**Duration of scene:** 4:15

---

**Summary of Movie:**
A hit man attends his 10th high school reunion. He intends to leave the ugly job behind and catch up with his old flame, but one last assignment ensnares him. This black comedy is worth viewing.

**Summary of Scene:**
Martin speaks to his psychiatrist, who does not say anything for awhile. Dr. Oatman finally says, "I'm not your doctor . . . Martin, I'm emotionally involved with you . . . I'm afraid of you and that constitutes emotional involvement, and it would be unethical for me to work with you under these circumstances." Martin says that Dr. Oatman got upset when Martin told him he was a hit man, and that Dr. Oatman let that knowledge "interfere with our dynamic." Dr. Oatman says that he does not want to work with Martin, but Martin "comes back every week at the same time." Dr. Oatman says that he would have to tell the authorities if Martin committed a crime or thought about committing a crime. Martin retorts that he is serious about getting therapy, and indirectly threatens Dr. Oatman by saying that he knows where he lives. Dr. Oatman gets more upset, says that he feels intimidated, and feels compelled to "be creative in a very interesting way, or else Martin will blow my brains out." Martin says, "What a person does for a living [doesn't] reflect who he is." Dr. Oatman becomes despondent, and tells Martin to go to his reunion. Martin likes the idea, and says, "I'll give it a shot."

## *Grosse Pointe Blank* : Insight Questions

Do you think that it is ethical and appropriate for a therapist to refuse to work with certain patients or clients?

Dr. Oatman says that he is emotionally involved with Martin? Is that true? If so, is that a good reason to end the therapeutic relationship?

Can a therapist work with a patient or client he or she is terrified of or intimidated by the patient?

Do mental health professionals have to tell authorities if their patient has committed a crime? Is it legal or ethical to do so?

Under what circumstances must a mental health professional inform authorities about a planned crime?

# *Grosse Pointe Blank*: Discussion Outline

### What do you make of Dr. Oatman's assertion that he and Martin are emotionally involved?

I agree with him. We sometimes assume that sexual relationships are the only hazardous ones in the field of mental health, but those involving danger and threats are also problematic. If you are afraid of a patient, then it is impossible to be effective.

### What are the hazards of being afraid of your patient?

As Dr. Oatman aptly points out later in the session, he feels compelled to be brilliant and creative, just to pacify his killer-patient. In that circumstance, he is not doing therapy with a clear head. At the end of the session Dr. Oatman looks hopeless and dejected, and starts to yell at his patient. I have told patients that I could not work with them if I feel scared. Usually, the fear involves their suicidal threats, and my statement is part of a dialogue in which I am explaining to a patient why he or she needs to go to the hospital (since I am too scared to treat him or her as an outpatient). However, there have been instances in which I have told patients that I could not work with them if they continued to intimidate me. I explain (trying to remain calm) that I will not make honest, blunt, or insightful comments if I am afraid of the consequences of doing so. Patients usually understand.

### Is it unethical to treat a patient whom you are afraid of?

As noted above, I think it is mostly a matter of effectiveness. I am not effective if I am afraid. I do not think it is an ethical issue.

### What do you say to a patient if you cannot treat him or her?

First, know your limitations. There may be some patients you cannot treat, such as child abusers (you may be too angry with them), people with certain political beliefs (strong right or left wing adherents may make you too upset), people with certain religious beliefs (which strongly conflict with your own beliefs), or others. If your list of people you cannot treat is too long, you may be too intolerant to be a therapist.

Second, tell the patient that it is your own problem (do not necessarily say why), and that you will help him or her to get another therapist. Try not to harm the patient in the process. Simply say that you are unable to treat him or her, and that he or she deserves therapy with someone who is better able to provide it.

*(continued on page 190)*

## Dr. Oatman says that he will inform authorities if Martin commits a crime. What is your reaction to that statement?

I do not agree. Except for child abuse, confidentiality laws prohibit disclosure of information to the authorities. I have had patients confess murder to me, and other crimes. I cannot inform authorities.

In the case of planned crimes, mental health professionals are bound to report if they believe their patients plan to harm a particular individual. But if the patient simply says that he has done despicable things in the past, the clinician must remain silent.

## Does Dr. Oatman act in such a way that we know that he cannot treat this patient?

Yes, he shows that because of his distress about treating a hit man, he is not effective as a therapist. First, he continues to see him even though he said he would not ("every week at the same time"). Second, he makes an erroneous statement about telling the authorities. Third, he is clearly most concerned with his own welfare (and not that of his patient) when he says, "Oh, that wasn't a nice thing to say. That wasn't designed to make me feel good." Fourth, he admits that he feels compelled to make certain "creative" and "really interesting" comments or interventions. Fifth, he makes desultory and disgusted comments by the end of the session when he asks Martin to describe his feelings, and when he tells him to go to the reunion. Sixth, he gets angry at his patient. Seventh, he gets alarmed at Martin's innocent comment, "Give it a shot."

## Why do so many films show psychiatrists in a bad light?

I believe that psychiatrists represent convenient vehicles for portraying someone who is controlling or befuddled, in the same way that Nazis or cowboys instantly conjure up certain stereotypes.

Many of the scenes are not realistic (including this one), but I laugh out loud every time I see this clip, as both actors are superb, and I love the dark humor.

# Analyze This

**Date of Movie:** 1999

**Actors in this scene:**
Billy Crystal as Dr. Ben Sobel
Molly Shannon as Caroline

**Timing on DVD:**
| | |
|---|---|
| 0:01:50 | Title |
| 0:05:29 | Start |
| 0:07:34 | End |

**Start of scene (VHS):** 0:03:39 after the title
Ben Sobel listens to Caroline. She reports that she told her husband that she needed room to grow.

**End of scene (VHS):** 0:05:44 after the title
The scene ends; Caroline weeps

**Duration of scene:** 2:55

---

**Summary of Movie:**
Dr. Ben Sobel, a psychiatrist, treats a Mafioso with panic attacks. Ben eventually joins the Mafia family, amidst domestic entanglements.

**Summary of Scene:**
Caroline feels awful that her husband left her. She believes that he did so because she expressed not only her womanhood, but also her personhood, her uniqueness and her independence. Amidst sobbing and blaming she wonders and wishes whether her husband will return to her. Ben interjects that he believes that it is unlikely that her husband will come back to her in light of the fact that he has taken out a restraining order. That comment fuels an additional outburst from Caroline, which in turn prompts Ben to imagine what he would like to say to her. He fantasizes telling her that she needs to "get a life" and stop whining. When Caroline arouses him from his daydreaming, he winds up the session with platitudes, implying that he looks forward to the next session. But when Ben mentions his upcoming vacation, Caroline gets hysterical, and says that he is just like her husband, who wants to get rid of her. His attempts to reassure her go awry - he tells her that he will only be gone for a week, while her husband will be gone forever.

191

## *Analyze This*: Insight Questions

Dr. Sobel looks bored in the session. Has a doctor ever seemed bored with you? How often do you think that doctors are bored, and not really interested in helping their patients?

Dr. Sobel mentions that her husband has taken out a restraining order, and that her husband does not want to see her ever again. Those comments seem to be blunt, and even cruel. Have you ever had experiences with doctors who are cruel or unkind?

In his daydream, Dr. Sobel tells Caroline to stop whining and to get a life. How could he tell her those thoughts in a way that is helpful and respectful?

If Dr. Sobel is bored with many of his patients, or disgusted with several of them, what should he do with his professional life? What does it mean to be burned out?

If a psychiatrist or a therapist has strong feelings toward one particular patient, and these feelings may interfere with the ability to care for that patient, what should the clinician do? How do you deal with distasteful patients? [See the scene from *Grosse Pointe Blank*, page 187]

## *Analyze This*: Discussion Outline

The director paints Caroline as a stereotypically distasteful patient. How does he do that?

- She is relatively unattractive
- Her clothes are not fashionable
- She is middle aged
- She is dependent
- She is self-centered
- She uses clichés
- She is oblivious to her effect on others
- She is histrionic; her gestures are overblown and comical

The first few times I watched the scene, I laughed at the pathetic patient. Later, I realized that Dr. Sobel is cruel. How do we know that Dr. Sobel is not in professional control?

As noted in the questions above, he mentions that her husband took out a restraining order and that he does not want to see her ever again. He says this in spite of the fact that Caroline hopes that her husband will return to her. Furthermore, he looks bored throughout the scene. In addition, Dr. Sobel's daydream is not only funny, but reveals that he is contemptuous and disgusted with Caroline. In other words, he not only has negative feelings for Caroline, but he acts them out.

Patients commonly feel transference for psychiatrists; they express feelings toward them that are parallel to other powerful feelings that they have. What transference do we notice in this scene? How could Dr. Sobel have used this transference reaction in a constructive manner?

Caroline feels abandoned by her husband, and she feels similarly abandoned by Dr. Sobel when he mentions going on vacation. In fact, she feels that he wants to discard her just as she feels discarded by her husband.

Dr. Sobel could have used their interchange in a more constructive manner. He could have pointed out the parallel between the two reactions, and he could ask her about feeling abandoned. He could ask whether she had a role in the process - did she provoke others to abandon her? That question could reverberate with the items noted in the first question - how does she turn people off, and how does she alienate people, including her husband (or therapist)? If Dr. Sobel raised those questions in a compassionate manner, she would be able to understand how her behavior is self-defeating. She could then modify her self-defeating behavior.

*(continued on page 194)*

## How do professionals know when they need help, and how do they get it?

I have two criteria for deciding when professionals need help. First, if the mental health professional *frequently* has negative feelings toward patients, or has one recurring feeling toward a variety of patients, then it is time for help. For example, the clinician is disgusted with many patients, or has sexual fantasies about many patients. Second, the clinician should get help if the reactions toward patients are acted upon. In this scene, Ben acts out his disgust toward Caroline when he makes cruel comments to her. Similarly, clinicians should get professional help if they notice that they take actions injurious to patients, for example:

- Forget appointments
- Make unkind remarks
- Flirt
- Discuss irrelevant topics
- Make unusual financial arrangements
- Overlook important material

The list could go on forever.

Once the clinician recognizes the need for help, then he or she should consult with colleagues if it is a relatively minor action, or get formal treatment to evaluate the underlying problem, if it is a more serious breach. The clinician may refrain from treating people until he or she rectifies the problem.

# Index

| Movie | Themes | Page # |
|---|---|---|
| *28 Days* | Alcohol and Drug Dependence, Enabling | 65 |
| *A Beautiful Mind* | Schizophrenia and Visual Hallucinations | 31 |
| *A Couch in New York* | Warmth and Caring Can Overcome Poor Technique | 175 |
| *Affliction* | Alcohol Dependence, Adult Child of Alcoholic | 77 |
| *Analyze This* | Psychiatrist Who Is Bored | 191 |
| *Anywhere But Here* | Histrionic Personality Traits | 101 |
| *As Good As It Gets* (1) | Obsessive-Compulsive Disorder | 55 |
| *As Good As It Gets* (2) | The Right Medicine and a Good Doctor-Patient Relationship | 151 |
| *Birdy* | Hospitalization | 147 |
| *Brassed Off* | Adjustment Disorder with Depressed Mood | 11 |
| *Broadcast News* (1) | Performance Anxiety | 47 |
| *Broadcast News* (2) | Obsessive-Compulsive Personality Disorder | 113 |
| *Caine Mutiny, The* | Paranoid Personality Disorder | 85 |
| *Cape Fear* | Antisocial Personality Disorder | 89 |
| *Clean and Sober* | A Sober Life | 73 |
| *Dressed to Kill* | Boundaries, Psychiatrist Who Is Too Involved | 179 |
| *E.T.* | Belief as a Therapeutic Tool | 157 |
| *Fatal Attraction* | Borderline Personality Disorder, Suicidal Behavior | 93 |
| *Fisher King, The* | Avoidant Personality Disorder, Dependency, Depression | 109 |
| *Four Weddings and a Funeral* | Performance Anxiety, Stage Fright & Shyness | 51 |
| *Frances* | The Patient Who Is Famous, Self-Centered Doctor | 183 |
| *Good Morning Vietnam* | Hypomania and Creativity | 25 |
| *Good Will Hunting* | Establishing the Doctor-Patient Relationship: Sincerity | 167 |
| *Graduate, The* | Coming of Age | 137 |
| *Grosse Point Blank* | Patient with Disturbing Background | 187 |
| *Hospital, The* | Depression, Alcohol Abuse, Family Conflict, Life Circumstances | 15 |
| *Last Days of Disco, The* | Narcissistic Personality Disorder | 105 |
| *Last Picture Show, The* | Major Depressive Disorder | 3 |
| *Lone Star* | Hypomanic Episode | 21 |
| *Manhattan Murder Mystery* | Panic Attack, Agoraphobia | 43 |
| *Midnight Run* | Panic Attack | 39 |
| *My Dinner With Andre* | Adult Developmental Issues, Intimacy, Fear of Death | 141 |
| *Ordinary People* (1) | Family Conflict | 133 |
| *Ordinary People* (2) | Establishing the Doctor-Patient Relationship: Genuineness | 171 |
| *Play Misty For Me* | Borderline Personality Disorder, Stalking | 97 |
| *Saving Private Ryan* | Grief and Forgetting | 119 |
| *Silence of the Lambs* | Establishing the Doctor-Patient Relationship: Honesty | 163 |
| *Smoke* | Pathological Grief, Visual Memories | 123 |
| *Straight Story, The* | Posttraumatic Stress Disorder and Substance Abuse | 59 |
| *Traffic* | Drug Dependence, Drugs and the Family | 69 |
| *Truly Madly Deeply* | Therapy for Pathological Grief | 127 |
| *Ulee's Gold* | Dysthymic Disorder | 7 |

a